LEARNING JAVASCRIPT FOR BEGINNERS

A Step-by-Step Guide to Mastering
JavaScript Fundamentals

THOMPSON CARTER

TABLE OF CONTENTS

Introduction

Welcome to *Learning JavaScript for Beginners: A Step-by-Step Guide to Mastering JavaScript Fundamentals*! Whether you're completely new to programming or coming from another language, this book is designed to guide you through the journey of mastering JavaScript, one of the most popular and versatile programming languages in the world today.

JavaScript has become a cornerstone of web development, enabling interactive and dynamic websites and applications. It's used by developers worldwide to create everything from small interactive forms to large-scale, complex applications. Originally developed for client-side web development, JavaScript has evolved into a powerful tool for both front-end and back-end development. With the rise of frameworks like **React**, **Vue**, and **Angular**, as well as server-side platforms like **Node.js**, JavaScript now powers full-stack applications, making it an essential skill for any developer.

This book is structured to take you from the very basics of JavaScript all the way to more advanced topics, ensuring you develop a deep understanding of the language. It's a comprehensive guide designed to break down complex concepts into easily digestible chunks, with clear explanations and hands-on examples. By the end of this book, you will have gained the confidence to write your own JavaScript programs and build web applications using JavaScript, whether on the client-side, server-side, or both.

What You Will Learn

Here's what you can expect to learn throughout the chapters of this book:

1. **The Basics of JavaScript**:
   - o You will start by understanding the fundamental concepts of JavaScript, such as variables, data types, operators, and control structures. This foundational knowledge is crucial for writing any JavaScript program.

2. **Functions and Scope**:
   - o Functions are the building blocks of JavaScript, and mastering them is essential. You will learn about function declarations, expressions, arrow functions, and how JavaScript handles **scope** and **closures**.

3. **Objects and Arrays**:
   - o JavaScript is an object-oriented language, and understanding how to work with **objects** and **arrays** is key to building dynamic applications. We will explore how to manipulate these data structures effectively.

4. **Asynchronous JavaScript**:

o Modern JavaScript heavily relies on asynchronous programming, especially for tasks like fetching data from APIs. You will learn about **callbacks**, **Promises**, and **async/await**, which are essential for handling asynchronous operations in JavaScript.

5. **DOM Manipulation**:

o One of JavaScript's primary uses is to interact with the **Document Object Model (DOM)**. This book will show you how to manipulate HTML elements dynamically, responding to user actions like clicks and form submissions.

6. **Working with APIs**:

o In today's web development, interacting with remote servers and fetching data is crucial. You'll learn how to make HTTP requests using JavaScript and handle data from **APIs**, which is fundamental for modern web applications.

7. **ES6+ Features**:

o JavaScript has evolved significantly in recent years with the introduction of **ES6** (ECMAScript 2015) and newer versions. Features like **template literals**, **destructuring, spread/rest operators**, and **modules** have made JavaScript more powerful and easier to work with. This book will cover these modern features to help you write cleaner and more efficient code.

8. **Advanced JavaScript Topics**:

   o Once you've covered the basics, we dive into more advanced topics such as **JavaScript closures, higher-order functions**, and **event delegation**. You'll also learn about important aspects of JavaScript such as **memory management** and **performance optimization**.

9. **Building Applications**:

   o We will guide you through building practical projects using JavaScript. By the end of the book, you'll have a complete understanding of how to apply your knowledge to real-world applications.

Why This Book?

- **Step-by-Step Approach**: Each chapter builds on the previous one, with examples and exercises designed to reinforce your understanding. Whether you're completely new to programming or have experience with other languages, the progression ensures you are always learning at a comfortable pace.

- **Hands-On Learning**: Learning by doing is the most effective way to master a programming language. This book is packed with coding examples, exercises, and projects that will help you apply what you've learned to real-world problems.

- **Jargon-Free Explanations**: We know that programming concepts can be intimidating at first, especially when they're filled with jargon. This book aims to keep things simple and jargon-free, making sure you understand the concepts in a way that is accessible and easy to grasp.

- **Real-World Examples**: From the very beginning, we'll focus on practical examples. You'll learn how to create interactive web pages, manage user input, work with APIs, and more. This hands-on approach prepares you for building your own projects as you advance.

- **Continued Learning**: JavaScript is an ever-evolving language, and this book provides resources to help you continue learning beyond the basics. Whether it's learning about the latest ECMAScript updates, exploring frameworks like React or Vue.js, or diving deeper into Node.js for backend development, we provide pathways for continued growth.

How This Book is Structured

This book is structured into 27 chapters, each focused on a specific aspect of JavaScript. Here's a brief breakdown:

- **Chapters 1-4**: Introduce the basics of JavaScript, including data types, operators, control flow, and functions.
- **Chapters 5-8**: Explore more complex topics like arrays, objects, DOM manipulation, and handling events.
- **Chapters 9-14**: Focus on more advanced JavaScript features, including ES6+ syntax, asynchronous programming, and working with APIs.
- **Chapters 15-20**: Cover more advanced JavaScript concepts such as closures, error handling, and memory management.
- **Chapters 21-26**: Focus on practical applications, including building web apps, working with frameworks like React, and diving into mobile development with React Native.
- **Chapter 27**: Concludes with the future of JavaScript and how to keep learning and improving your skills.

Who This Book Is For

This book is ideal for beginners who are eager to learn JavaScript from scratch. Whether you're interested in becoming a front-end web developer, a full-stack developer, or even a mobile app developer, mastering JavaScript is essential. If you're already familiar with basic programming concepts but new to JavaScript, this book will help you quickly get up to speed with the language and start building real-world projects.

Getting Started

Ready to dive in? Let's begin our journey into JavaScript! Throughout this book, you'll encounter explanations, code examples, and practical exercises that will help you not only understand but also enjoy learning JavaScript. By the end of this book, you'll have the skills and confidence to tackle more advanced topics, contribute to open-source projects, and build your own JavaScript applications.

Let's get started on your path to mastering JavaScript!

Chapter 1: Introduction to JavaScript

Overview of JavaScript and its Role in Web Development

JavaScript is a dynamic and versatile programming language primarily used to add interactivity and functionality to websites. It is an essential part of the web development triad, alongside HTML (HyperText Markup Language) and CSS (Cascading Style Sheets). While HTML structures a webpage and CSS controls its presentation, JavaScript brings the page to life with dynamic behavior and responsiveness. With JavaScript, you can handle events like user clicks, form submissions, animations, and much more.

The primary role of JavaScript in web development includes:

- **Client-side scripting:** JavaScript executes directly in the user's browser, enabling fast and efficient updates to the page without needing to reload it. This enhances user experience and interactivity.
- **Server-side scripting:** With environments like Node.js, JavaScript can also run on the server to build web applications and APIs.
- **Web APIs and integration:** JavaScript can interact with web APIs (Application Programming Interfaces) to fetch

and display data from external servers, helping developers create modern, data-driven applications.

History and Evolution of JavaScript

JavaScript was created by **Brendan Eich** in 1995 while working at Netscape Communications. Initially called **Mocha**, the language was renamed **LiveScript** before ultimately being called **JavaScript**. It was designed to be a lightweight, interpreted language that could run in the browser, complementing the static nature of HTML.

The evolution of JavaScript has been marked by several key milestones:

- **1995:** Creation of JavaScript by Brendan Eich at Netscape Communications.
- **1997:** JavaScript was standardized by ECMA International as **ECMAScript**, which allowed the language to be more universally accepted and consistent across different browsers.
- **2005:** The rise of **AJAX (Asynchronous JavaScript and XML)** marked a turning point, enabling dynamic page updates and the birth of modern web applications.
- **2009: Node.js** brought JavaScript to the server, allowing developers to build scalable network applications with JavaScript.

- **2015:** ECMAScript 6 (ES6) introduced significant improvements to the language, including **let/const**, **arrow functions**, **classes**, **template literals**, and more, making JavaScript a more powerful and modern language.

Today, JavaScript is one of the most widely used programming languages in the world, powering a vast range of applications, from simple websites to complex web platforms, mobile apps, and server-side systems.

Setting up the Development Environment (IDE, Browser Dev Tools)

Before diving into coding, it's essential to set up your development environment. You'll need an **IDE (Integrated Development Environment)** and the **browser's developer tools** to run and test JavaScript code efficiently.

1. **Choosing an IDE:** An IDE is a software application that provides comprehensive tools for writing, editing, and testing code. For JavaScript, some of the most popular IDEs and text editors are:
    - **Visual Studio Code (VSCode):** A free, open-source, and highly extensible IDE with excellent JavaScript support, syntax highlighting, and debugging tools.
    - **Sublime Text:** A lightweight and fast text editor with JavaScript syntax support.

- o **Atom:** Another open-source text editor that's easy to customize and offers JavaScript support.

These IDEs often include features such as **auto-completion**, **syntax highlighting**, **debugging tools**, and **extensions** that enhance productivity.

2. **Browser Developer Tools:** All modern web browsers (Chrome, Firefox, Edge, etc.) come with built-in **developer tools** that allow you to inspect the HTML structure, view console logs, and test JavaScript directly in the browser. You can access these tools by pressing **F12** or **Ctrl+Shift+I**.
   - o **Console Tab:** This is where you can directly write and test JavaScript code. It's useful for experimenting with code snippets and seeing how the browser responds.
   - o **Elements Tab:** Here, you can inspect the DOM structure of the webpage, modify elements, and see how your JavaScript manipulates the page in real-time.
   - o **Network Tab:** Use this to monitor network requests and responses, especially when dealing with API calls and asynchronous code.

Your First JavaScript Program: "Hello, World!"

To start programming in JavaScript, we'll create a simple program that displays **"Hello, World!"** in the browser. This is the classic first program for many new programmers.

Step 1: Writing the HTML

First, you'll need an HTML file where your JavaScript code will live. You can write the JavaScript inside the HTML file using the <script> tag.

Create a new file called index.html and add the following content:

html

```
<!DOCTYPE html>
<html lang="en">
<head>
   <meta charset="UTF-8">
   <meta name="viewport" content="width=device-width, initial-scale=1.0">
   <title>First JavaScript Program</title>
</head>
<body>
   <h1>Welcome to JavaScript Programming</h1>

   <script>
     // JavaScript code goes here
     console.log("Hello, World!");
   </script>
</body>
</html>
```

Step 2: Opening the HTML File in the Browser

Once you've saved the file, open it in your web browser by double-clicking the index.html file. Then, press **F12** to open the browser's developer tools and navigate to the **Console** tab. You should see the message:

Hello, World!

This simple JavaScript code prints the text "Hello, World!" to the console using console.log(). The **console** is a common tool used to display output, debug code, and check for errors during development.

In this chapter, you've learned about the role of JavaScript in web development, its evolution, how to set up your development environment, and created your first JavaScript program. As you move forward in this guide, you'll build on these foundations to learn more advanced topics and start writing more dynamic code!

Chapter 2: Variables and Data Types

Understanding Variables: var, let, and const

In JavaScript, variables are used to store data that can be accessed and manipulated later. JavaScript has three ways to declare variables: var, let, and const. Each of these has different use cases and scoping rules.

1. **var**:

    o var was the original way to declare variables in JavaScript. However, it has some quirks that led to the introduction of let and const. The primary issue with var is that it is **function-scoped**, meaning it is available throughout the entire function in which it is declared (even if declared inside a block like a loop or an if statement).

    o **Example:**

    javascript

    ```javascript
    var name = "John";
    if (true) {
        var name = "Jane";
    }
    console.log(name); // Output: "Jane"
    ```

2. **let**:

○ Introduced in **ES6 (ECMAScript 2015)**, let allows you to declare variables with **block-level scope**, meaning they are only available within the block (e.g., loops or conditionals) where they are defined.

○ **Example:**

javascript

```
let age = 25;
if (true) {
    let age = 30;
    console.log(age); // Output: 30 (within block)
}
console.log(age); // Output: 25 (outside block)
```

3. **const**:

○ const is used to declare variables whose values cannot be reassigned after initialization. It also follows **block-level scope** like let. However, it's important to note that while const prevents reassignment of the variable, it does not make objects or arrays immutable (i.e., their properties or elements can still be changed).

○ **Example:**

javascript

```
const city = "New York";
// city = "Los Angeles"; // Error: Assignment to constant
variable
```

```
const person = { name: "Alice" };
person.name = "Bob"; // This is allowed, as the object itself is
not immutable.
console.log(person.name); // Output: "Bob"
```

Primitive Data Types

Primitive data types represent simple values and are immutable. JavaScript has six primitive data types:

1. **String**:
   - A string is a sequence of characters wrapped in single quotes ('), double quotes ("), or backticks (`).
   - **Example:**

     javascript

     ```
     let greeting = "Hello, world!";
     let name = 'John Doe';
     let message = `Welcome, ${name}!`;
     console.log(greeting); // Output: Hello, world!
     ```

2. **Number**:
   - Numbers in JavaScript are not divided into integer and floating-point types. They can represent both whole numbers and decimals.

- o **Example:**

  javascript

  ```
  let age = 30;
  let price = 19.99;
  let result = age + price;
  console.log(result); // Output: 49.99
  ```

3. **Boolean**:
   - o A boolean value can either be true or false. Booleans are often used in conditionals and control flow.
   - o **Example:**

     javascript

     ```
     let isActive = true;
     let hasPermission = false;
     console.log(isActive); // Output: true
     ```

4. **Null**:
   - o The null value represents the intentional absence of any object value. It is often used to indicate that a variable is intentionally empty.
   - o **Example:**

     javascript

     ```
     let user = null;
     ```

```
console.log(user); // Output: null
```

5. **Undefined**:
   - A variable that has been declared but not assigned a value has the value undefined. It is the default value assigned to uninitialized variables.
   - **Example:**

   javascript

   ```
   let x;
   console.log(x); // Output: undefined
   ```

6. **Symbol (ES6)**:
   - Symbols are a unique and immutable data type used primarily for object property keys. They are not commonly used for beginners but are useful in more advanced JavaScript patterns.
   - **Example:**

   javascript

   ```
   const sym = Symbol('description');
   console.log(sym); // Output: Symbol(description)
   ```

Complex Data Types

While primitive types are immutable, complex data types in JavaScript are mutable and can hold more complex structures.

1. **Objects**:
   - Objects in JavaScript are collections of key-value pairs, where the key is always a string (or symbol), and the value can be any data type.
   - **Example:**

   javascript

   ```javascript
   let person = {
       name: "Alice",
       age: 28,
       greet: function() {
           console.log("Hello, " + this.name);
       }
   };
   person.greet(); // Output: Hello, Alice
   ```

2. **Arrays**:
   - Arrays are ordered collections of values, which can be of any data type. Arrays can store multiple values in a single variable, making them very useful for managing lists of data.
   - **Example:**

   javascript

   ```javascript
   let fruits = ["apple", "banana", "cherry"];
   console.log(fruits[0]); // Output: apple
   fruits.push("orange");
   ```

console.log(fruits); // Output: ["apple", "banana", "cherry", "orange"]

Type Coercion and Type Checking

JavaScript performs **type coercion**, meaning it automatically converts one data type to another when necessary. This can sometimes lead to unexpected results.

1. **Type Coercion**:
   o JavaScript can automatically convert a string to a number or a number to a string in certain operations.
   o **Example:**

   javascript

   ```javascript
   let result = "5" + 2; // "52" (string concatenation)
   console.log(result);

   let sum = "5" - 2; // 3 (coerces "5" to a number)
   console.log(sum);
   ```

2. **Type Checking**:
   o Use typeof to check the type of a variable.
   o **Example:**

   javascript

   ```javascript
   let num = 42;
   console.log(typeof num); // Output: number
   ```

```javascript
let message = "Hello";
console.log(typeof message); // Output: string
```

```javascript
let isActive = true;
console.log(typeof isActive); // Output: boolean
```

- o For more complex data types (e.g., objects, arrays), typeof may not always provide the expected results, so you may use Array.isArray() for arrays.
- o **Example:**

javascript

```javascript
let array = [1, 2, 3];
console.log(Array.isArray(array)); // Output: true
```

3. **Strict Equality (===) vs. Loose Equality (==):**
   - o The **strict equality operator (===)** compares both the value and the type, while the **loose equality operator (==)** converts types before comparing.
   - o **Example:**

javascript

```javascript
let x = "5";
let y = 5;
```

```javascript
console.log(x == y); // Output: true (type coercion)
```

```
console.log(x === y); // Output: false (no type coercion)
```

In this chapter, you've learned how to work with **variables** and **data types** in JavaScript, understanding the differences between var, let, and const, as well as how to use both primitive and complex data types. You've also explored **type coercion** and **type checking**, both essential concepts to keep in mind as you write JavaScript code. These foundations will help you handle data efficiently as you progress in your journey to mastering JavaScript.

Chapter 3: Operators in JavaScript

Arithmetic, Assignment, and Comparison Operators

JavaScript provides a variety of operators for performing operations on variables and values. These operators can be categorized into **arithmetic**, **assignment**, and **comparison** operators.

1. **Arithmetic Operators**: Arithmetic operators are used to perform basic mathematical operations.

   o **Addition (+)**: Adds two numbers.

   javascript

   ```javascript
   let sum = 5 + 3;
   console.log(sum); // Output: 8
   ```

   o **Subtraction (-)**: Subtracts one number from another.

   javascript

   ```javascript
   let difference = 10 - 4;
   console.log(difference); // Output: 6
   ```

   o **Multiplication (*)**: Multiplies two numbers.

   javascript

```javascript
let product = 4 * 7;
console.log(product); // Output: 28
```

- Division (/): Divides one number by another.

javascript

```javascript
let quotient = 20 / 4;
console.log(quotient); // Output: 5
```

- **Modulus (%)**: Returns the remainder of a division operation.

javascript

```javascript
let remainder = 17 % 5;
console.log(remainder); // Output: 2
```

- **Exponentiation (**)**: Raises the first operand to the power of the second operand.

javascript

```javascript
let power = 2 ** 3;
console.log(power); // Output: 8
```

2. **Assignment Operators**: Assignment operators are used to assign values to variables. The most common is the simple = assignment, but there are several compound assignment operators that combine an operation with an assignment.

o **Simple Assignment (=)**: Assigns the right operand to the left operand.

javascript

```
let x = 10;
console.log(x); // Output: 10
```

o **Add Assignment (+=)**: Adds the right operand to the left operand and assigns the result to the left operand.

javascript

```
let y = 5;
y += 3; // Equivalent to y = y + 3
console.log(y); // Output: 8
```

o **Subtract Assignment (-=)**: Subtracts the right operand from the left operand and assigns the result to the left operand.

javascript

```
let z = 10;
z -= 2; // Equivalent to z = z - 2
console.log(z); // Output: 8
```

○ **Multiply Assignment (*=)**: Multiplies the left operand by the right operand and assigns the result to the left operand.

javascript

```
let a = 4;
a *= 2; // Equivalent to a = a * 2
console.log(a); // Output: 8
```

○ **Divide Assignment (/=)**: Divides the left operand by the right operand and assigns the result to the left operand.

javascript

```
let b = 10;
b /= 2; // Equivalent to b = b / 2
console.log(b); // Output: 5
```

○ **Modulus Assignment (%=)**: Takes the modulus of the left operand by the right operand and assigns the result to the left operand.

javascript

```
let c = 15;
c %= 4; // Equivalent to c = c % 4
console.log(c); // Output: 3
```

3. **Comparison Operators**: Comparison operators are used to compare two values. They return a boolean value (true or false).

- ○ **Equal to (==)**: Compares two values for equality, ignoring the data type.

  javascript

  ```javascript
  let a = 5;
  let b = '5';
  console.log(a == b); // Output: true (type coercion occurs)
  ```

- ○ **Strict Equal to (===)**: Compares both value and type for equality.

  javascript

  ```javascript
  let a = 5;
  let b = '5';
  console.log(a === b); // Output: false (no type coercion)
  ```

- ○ **Not Equal to (!=)**: Checks if two values are not equal.

  javascript

  ```javascript
  let a = 5;
  let b = 6;
  console.log(a != b); // Output: true
  ```

o **Strict Not Equal to (!==)**: Checks if two values are not equal, considering both value and type.

javascript

```
let a = 5;
let b = '5';
console.log(a !== b); // Output: true
```

o **Greater than (>)**: Checks if the left operand is greater than the right operand.

javascript

```
let a = 7;
let b = 5;
console.log(a > b); // Output: true
```

o **Less than (<)**: Checks if the left operand is less than the right operand.

javascript

```
let a = 3;
let b = 5;
console.log(a < b); // Output: true
```

o **Greater than or Equal to (>=)**: Checks if the left operand is greater than or equal to the right operand.

javascript

```
let a = 5;
let b = 5;
console.log(a >= b); // Output: true
```

○ **Less than or Equal to (<=)**: Checks if the left operand is less than or equal to the right operand.

javascript

```
let a = 4;
let b = 5;
console.log(a <= b); // Output: true
```

Logical Operators

Logical operators are used to combine two or more conditions. They return a boolean value (true or false).

1. **AND (&&)**:
   ○ Returns true if both operands are true, otherwise returns false.
   ○ **Example:**

   javascript

   ```
   let a = true;
   let b = false;
   console.log(a && b); // Output: false
   ```

2. **OR (||):**

   o Returns true if at least one operand is true, otherwise returns false.

   o **Example:**

   javascript

   ```
   let a = true;
   let b = false;
   console.log(a || b); // Output: true
   ```

3. **NOT (!):**

   o Inverts the boolean value of its operand. If the operand is true, it returns false, and if it is false, it returns true.

   o **Example:**

   javascript

   ```
   let a = true;
   console.log(!a); // Output: false
   ```

Ternary Operator

The ternary operator is a shorthand for an if-else statement. It takes three operands:

- A condition (expression to evaluate)
- A value to return if the condition is true

- A value to return if the condition is false

The syntax is:

javascript

condition ? value_if_true : value_if_false;

Example:

javascript

```
let age = 18;
let result = age >= 18 ? "Adult" : "Minor";
console.log(result); // Output: Adult
```

Operator Precedence and Associativity

Operator precedence determines the order in which operators are evaluated in an expression. Operators with higher precedence are evaluated first. For example, multiplication (*) has a higher precedence than addition (+).

1. **Precedence**:
   - Arithmetic operators (*, /, %) have higher precedence than addition and subtraction (+, -).
   - Comparison operators (==, !=, >, <) have lower precedence than arithmetic operators.

   Example:

   javascript

```
let result = 5 + 3 * 2;
console.log(result); // Output: 11 (multiplication happens first)
```

2. **Associativity**:

   o Most operators have **left-to-right** associativity, meaning they are evaluated from left to right.

   o **Example**: 5 - 2 - 1 is evaluated as (5 - 2) - 1.

   o Some operators, like the assignment operator (=), have **right-to-left** associativity.

   o **Example**:

   javascript

   ```
   let a, b, c;
   a = b = c = 5;
   console.log(a); // Output: 5
   ```

In this chapter, you learned about **arithmetic, assignment,** and **comparison operators**, as well as **logical operators** that help control the flow of your code. You also explored the **ternary operator** as a concise way to express conditional logic and learned about **operator precedence** and **associativity** to control the order of evaluation in your expressions. Understanding these operators is fundamental to writing efficient and effective JavaScript code.

Chapter 4: Control Flow Statements

Control flow statements in JavaScript allow you to control the flow of execution of your code based on certain conditions. These statements enable you to make decisions, repeat actions, and control the behavior of your program. The main types of control flow statements are **conditional statements**, **loops**, and **loop control statements**.

Conditional Statements: if, else, switch

1. **if Statement**: The if statement is the most basic control flow statement, used to execute a block of code if a condition is true.

   Syntax:

   javascript

   ```javascript
   if (condition) {
       // code to execute if condition is true
   }
   ```
   Example:

   javascript

```
let age = 18;
if (age >= 18) {
    console.log("You are an adult.");
}
// Output: You are an adult.
```

2. **else Statement**: The else statement provides an alternative block of code that runs if the condition in the if statement is false.

    Syntax:

    javascript

    ```
    if (condition) {
        // code if condition is true
    } else {
        // code if condition is false
    }
    ```

    Example:

    javascript

    ```
    let age = 16;
    if (age >= 18) {
        console.log("You are an adult.");
    } else {
        console.log("You are a minor.");
    }
    ```

// Output: You are a minor.

3. **else if Statement**: The else if statement allows you to check multiple conditions in sequence. If the first if condition is false, it checks the else if condition, and so on.

Syntax:

javascript

```
if (condition1) {
    // code if condition1 is true
} else if (condition2) {
    // code if condition2 is true
} else {
    // code if no condition is true
}
```

Example:

javascript

```
let age = 20;
if (age < 13) {
    console.log("Child");
} else if (age < 18) {
    console.log("Teenager");
} else {
    console.log("Adult");
}
// Output: Adult
```

4. **switch Statement**: The switch statement is used to perform a multi-way branch. It compares the expression with multiple cases and executes the code block associated with the matching case.

Syntax:

javascript

```
switch (expression) {
    case value1:
        // code for value1
        break;
    case value2:
        // code for value2
        break;
    default:
        // code if no case matches
}
```

Example:

javascript

```
let day = 3;
switch (day) {
    case 1:
        console.log("Monday");
        break;
    case 2:
        console.log("Tuesday");
```

```
      break;
  case 3:
      console.log("Wednesday");
      break;
  default:
      console.log("Invalid day");
}
// Output: Wednesday
```

- o The break statement is important in switch to exit the switch block once a matching case is found. If omitted, the execution will continue to the next case (this is called **fall-through** behavior).

Logical Operators and Combining Conditions

Logical operators allow you to combine multiple conditions into one and make complex decisions in your code.

1. **AND (&&):**
   - o Returns true if both conditions are true.
   - o **Example:**

   javascript

   ```
   let age = 25;
   let hasLicense = true;
   if (age >= 18 && hasLicense) {
   ```

```javascript
      console.log("You can drive.");
    } else {
      console.log("You cannot drive.");
    }
    // Output: You can drive.
```

2. **OR (||):**

   o   Returns true if at least one condition is true.

   o   **Example**:

   javascript

```javascript
    let age = 16;
    let hasParentalConsent = true;
    if (age >= 18 || hasParentalConsent) {
      console.log("You can sign up.");
    } else {
      console.log("You cannot sign up.");
    }
    // Output: You can sign up.
```

3. **NOT (!):**

   o   Inverts the boolean value of a condition. If the condition is true, it returns false, and if the condition is false, it returns true.

   o   **Example**:

   javascript

```javascript
let isActive = false;
if (!isActive) {
    console.log("Account is inactive.");
}
// Output: Account is inactive.
```

You can combine multiple logical operators to form more complex conditions:

javascript

```javascript
let age = 20;
let hasMembership = true;
if (age >= 18 && (hasMembership || age > 60)) {
    console.log("Eligible for a discount.");
} else {
    console.log("Not eligible for a discount.");
}
// Output: Eligible for a discount.
```

Loops: for, while, do...while

Loops are used to repeatedly execute a block of code until a specified condition is met. JavaScript provides three types of loops: for, while, and do...while.

1. **for Loop**: The for loop is used when you know in advance how many times the code block should be executed.

   Syntax:

javascript

```
for (initialization; condition; increment) {
    // code to be executed
}
```

Example:

javascript

```
for (let i = 0; i < 5; i++) {
    console.log(i);
}
// Output: 0 1 2 3 4
```

2. **while Loop**: The while loop continues to execute as long as the specified condition evaluates to true. The condition is checked before each iteration.

Syntax:

javascript

```
while (condition) {
    // code to be executed
}
```

Example:

javascript

```
let i = 0;
while (i < 5) {
```

```
    console.log(i);
     i++;
}
// Output: 0 1 2 3 4
```

3. **do...while Loop**: The do...while loop is similar to the while loop, but the condition is checked after the block of code is executed. This ensures that the loop executes at least once.

   Syntax:

   javascript

   ```
   do {
       // code to be executed
   } while (condition);
   ```
   Example:

   javascript

   ```
   let i = 0;
   do {
       console.log(i);
        i++;
   } while (i < 5);
   // Output: 0 1 2 3 4
   ```

Breaking Out of Loops (break, continue)

Sometimes, you need to exit a loop prematurely or skip certain iterations. JavaScript provides two control statements for this: break and continue.

1. **break Statement**: The break statement is used to immediately exit a loop (or a switch case) and stop further iterations.

   Example:

   javascript

   ```
   for (let i = 0; i < 5; i++) {
       if (i === 3) {
           break; // Exits the loop when i equals 3
       }
       console.log(i);
   }
   // Output: 0 1 2
   ```

2. **continue Statement**: The continue statement is used to skip the current iteration of a loop and move to the next iteration.

   Example:

   javascript

   ```
   for (let i = 0; i < 5; i++) {
       if (i === 2) {
           continue; // Skips the iteration when i equals 2
   ```

```
    }
    console.log(i);
}
// Output: 0 1 3 4
```

In this chapter, you've learned about **conditional statements** (if, else, switch), **logical operators** for combining conditions, and the various types of **loops** (for, while, do...while). You've also explored how to control the flow of loops using break and continue. These control flow tools are fundamental to writing efficient and logical JavaScript code, allowing you to build dynamic and interactive applications.

Chapter 5: Functions in JavaScript

Functions are fundamental building blocks in JavaScript. They allow you to group code into reusable blocks, making your program more organized and efficient. This chapter covers how to define functions, use parameters and return values, and explore different types of functions in JavaScript, including **arrow functions** and **anonymous functions**. We'll also delve into the important concepts of **scope** and **closure**.

Defining Functions: Function Declaration vs. Function Expression

In JavaScript, there are two primary ways to define functions: **function declaration** and **function expression**.

1. **Function Declaration**: A function declaration defines a named function. It is hoisted, meaning it can be called before it is defined in the code.

   Syntax:

   javascript

   function functionName() {

```
// code to be executed
}
```

Example:

javascript

```
function greet() {
    console.log("Hello, World!");
}
greet(); // Output: Hello, World!
```

- o Function declarations are hoisted, meaning you can call the function before its definition in the code.

Example of hoisting:

javascript

```
greet(); // Output: Hello, World!
function greet() {
    console.log("Hello, World!");
}
```

2. **Function Expression**: A function expression defines a function as part of an expression. Function expressions are not hoisted, meaning they must be defined before being called.

Syntax:

javascript

```
const functionName = function() {
    // code to be executed
};
```

Example:

javascript

```
const greet = function() {
    console.log("Hello, World!");
};
greet(); // Output: Hello, World!
```

- o Function expressions can be anonymous, meaning they do not have a name.

Function Parameters and Return Values

Functions can accept **parameters**, which are values passed into the function when it is called. Functions can also **return values** after performing some operations.

1. **Function Parameters**:
   - o Parameters are variables that are used to pass values into a function when it is called.
   - o A function can accept multiple parameters, and they can be of any data type.

Example:

javascript

```
function add(a, b) {
   return a + b;
}
let result = add(5, 3); // Arguments passed: 5 and 3
console.log(result); // Output: 8
```

- o   If a function does not have a return statement, it implicitly returns undefined.

Example:

javascript

```
function greet(name) {
   console.log("Hello, " + name);
}
greet("Alice"); // Output: Hello, Alice
```

2. **Return Values**:
   - o   A function can return a value using the return keyword. Once a return statement is executed, the function exits, and the value is returned to the caller.

Example:

javascript

```
function multiply(a, b) {
    return a * b;
}
let result = multiply(4, 5);
console.log(result); // Output: 20
```

Arrow Functions and Anonymous Functions

1. **Arrow Functions**: Arrow functions are a more concise way to define functions, introduced in **ES6 (ECMAScript 2015)**. They are also known as **fat arrow functions** due to the => syntax.

    o   Arrow functions are **anonymous** functions, meaning they do not require a name.

    o   They also have a **lexical this**, meaning this refers to the context in which the arrow function was created, unlike regular functions that have their own this.

Syntax:

javascript

```
const functionName = (parameters) => {
    // code to be executed
};
```

Example (single parameter, implicit return):

javascript

```
const greet = name => console.log("Hello, " + name);
greet("Alice"); // Output: Hello, Alice
```

Example (multiple parameters, explicit return):

javascript

```
const add = (a, b) => {
    return a + b;
};
let result = add(3, 4);
console.log(result); // Output: 7
```

2. **Anonymous Functions**: Anonymous functions are functions without a name. They are often used as function expressions or passed as arguments to other functions.

Example:

javascript

```
setTimeout(function() {
    console.log("This message is displayed after 2 seconds.");
}, 2000);
```

o   In this example, the function passed to setTimeout is an anonymous function.

Understanding Scope and Closure

1. **Scope**: Scope refers to the context in which a variable or function is accessible. JavaScript has **global scope** and **local scope**. Variables declared inside a function have **local scope**, while variables declared outside any function have **global scope**.

    o **Global Scope**: Variables declared outside any function are accessible from anywhere in the code.

    o **Local Scope**: Variables declared inside a function are only accessible within that function.

    Example:

    javascript

    ```javascript
    let globalVar = "I am global";

    function myFunction() {
        let localVar = "I am local";
        console.log(globalVar); // Can access global variable
        console.log(localVar); // Can access local variable
    }

    myFunction();
    console.log(globalVar); // Output: I am global
    // console.log(localVar); // Error: localVar is not defined
    ```

2. **Closure**: A **closure** occurs when a function retains access to the variables from its outer scope, even after the outer function has finished executing. Closures are created every time a function is defined within another function.

Example:

javascript

```
function outerFunction() {
    let outerVar = "I am outside!";
    function innerFunction() {
        console.log(outerVar); // The inner function retains access to
outerVar
    }
    return innerFunction;
}

const closureFunc = outerFunction();
closureFunc(); // Output: I am outside!
```

- o In this example, innerFunction has access to the variable outerVar from the outer function, even though outerFunction has finished executing.
- o Closures are especially useful when working with callbacks or functions that maintain state over time.

In this chapter, you've learned how to define and use functions in JavaScript, including **function declarations** and **function expressions**. You've explored **arrow functions** and **anonymous functions**, and how they differ from traditional functions. Additionally, you've understood the important concepts of **scope** and **closure**, which help manage variable visibility and maintain the integrity of your code. Functions are powerful tools in JavaScript, enabling modular, reusable, and maintainable code.

Chapter 6: Arrays and Array Methods

Arrays are one of the most commonly used data structures in JavaScript. They allow you to store multiple values in a single variable, which makes working with lists of data efficient. In this chapter, we'll explore how to create and manipulate arrays, how to access and iterate through array elements, and the various array methods that allow for advanced operations on arrays. We'll also discuss multi-dimensional arrays, which are arrays of arrays.

Creating and Manipulating Arrays

1. **Creating Arrays**: Arrays can be created in JavaScript using either the array literal syntax or the Array constructor.

   o **Array Literal**: The most common and preferred way to create an array is by using square brackets [].

   Example:

   javascript

   ```javascript
   let fruits = ["apple", "banana", "cherry"];
   console.log(fruits); // Output: ["apple", "banana", "cherry"]
   ```

o **Array Constructor**: You can also create an array using the Array constructor, though this is less commonly used.

Example:

javascript

```
let numbers = new Array(1, 2, 3, 4, 5);
console.log(numbers); // Output: [1, 2, 3, 4, 5]
```

2. **Manipulating Arrays**: You can add, remove, or change elements in an array using various methods.

o **Changing elements**: Arrays are mutable, meaning you can change elements at any index.

Example:

javascript

```
let fruits = ["apple", "banana", "cherry"];
fruits[1] = "blueberry"; // Changing "banana" to "blueberry"
console.log(fruits); // Output: ["apple", "blueberry", "cherry"]
```

o **Adding elements**: You can add elements to the end or the beginning of an array using push() or unshift() respectively.

Example:

javascript

```
let fruits = ["apple", "banana"];
fruits.push("cherry"); // Adds "cherry" to the end of the array
console.log(fruits); // Output: ["apple", "banana", "cherry"]

fruits.unshift("grape"); // Adds "grape" to the beginning of the array
console.log(fruits); // Output: ["grape", "apple", "banana", "cherry"]
```

- o **Removing elements**: You can remove elements from the end or the beginning of an array using pop() or shift() respectively.

Example:

javascript

```
let fruits = ["apple", "banana", "cherry"];
let lastFruit = fruits.pop(); // Removes the last element
console.log(lastFruit); // Output: "cherry"
console.log(fruits); // Output: ["apple", "banana"]

let firstFruit = fruits.shift(); // Removes the first element
console.log(firstFruit); // Output: "apple"
console.log(fruits); // Output: ["banana"]
```

Accessing Array Elements and Iterating Through Arrays

1. **Accessing Array Elements**: You can access individual elements of an array using an index. Array indices are zero-based, meaning the first element has an index of 0.

   Example:

   javascript

   ```javascript
   let fruits = ["apple", "banana", "cherry"];
   console.log(fruits[0]); // Output: "apple"
   console.log(fruits[2]); // Output: "cherry"
   ```

2. **Iterating Through Arrays**: There are several ways to loop through arrays to process each element.

   o **Using a for loop**: You can use a for loop to iterate through the array and access each element by its index.

   Example:

   javascript

   ```javascript
   let fruits = ["apple", "banana", "cherry"];
   for (let i = 0; i < fruits.length; i++) {
       console.log(fruits[i]);
   }
   // Output: apple, banana, cherry
   ```

o **Using forEach method**: The forEach() method allows you to iterate over each element in the array, applying a function to each element.

Example:

javascript

```
let fruits = ["apple", "banana", "cherry"];
fruits.forEach(function(fruit) {
    console.log(fruit);
});
// Output: apple, banana, cherry
```

Array Methods

JavaScript provides several built-in methods that allow you to perform operations on arrays. These methods are essential for manipulating and transforming array data.

1. **push()**: Adds one or more elements to the end of an array.

Example:

javascript

```
let fruits = ["apple", "banana"];
fruits.push("cherry", "date");
console.log(fruits); // Output: ["apple", "banana", "cherry", "date"]
```

2. **pop()**: Removes the last element from an array.

   Example:

   javascript

   ```javascript
   let fruits = ["apple", "banana", "cherry"];
   fruits.pop();
   console.log(fruits); // Output: ["apple", "banana"]
   ```

3. **shift()**: Removes the first element from an array.

   Example:

   javascript

   ```javascript
   let fruits = ["apple", "banana", "cherry"];
   fruits.shift();
   console.log(fruits); // Output: ["banana", "cherry"]
   ```

4. **unshift()**: Adds one or more elements to the beginning of an array.

   Example:

   javascript

   ```javascript
   let fruits = ["banana", "cherry"];
   fruits.unshift("apple");
   console.log(fruits); // Output: ["apple", "banana", "cherry"]
   ```

5. **slice()**: Returns a shallow of a portion of an array, without modifying the original array.

   Example:

   javascript

   ```
   let fruits = ["apple", "banana", "cherry", "date"];
   let slicedFruits = fruits.slice(1, 3); // Extracts from index 1 to index 2
   console.log(slicedFruits); // Output: ["banana", "cherry"]
   console.log(fruits); // Output: ["apple", "banana", "cherry", "date"]
   ```

6. **splice()**: Changes the contents of an array by removing or replacing existing elements and/or adding new elements.

   Example:

   javascript

   ```
   let fruits = ["apple", "banana", "cherry"];
   fruits.splice(1, 1, "blueberry", "date"); // Removes 1 element at index 1
   and adds "blueberry" and "date"
   console.log(fruits); // Output: ["apple", "blueberry", "date", "cherry"]
   ```

7. **map()**: Creates a new array by applying a function to each element in the original array.

   Example:

   javascript

```javascript
let numbers = [1, 2, 3, 4];
let squaredNumbers = numbers.map(function(num) {
    return num * num;
});
console.log(squaredNumbers); // Output: [1, 4, 9, 16]
```

8. **filter()**: Creates a new array with all elements that pass a test defined by a function.

   Example:

   javascript

```javascript
let numbers = [1, 2, 3, 4, 5];
let evenNumbers = numbers.filter(function(num) {
    return num % 2 === 0;
});
console.log(evenNumbers); // Output: [2, 4]
```

9. **reduce()**: Applies a function to each element in the array (from left to right) to reduce it to a single value.

   Example:

   javascript

```javascript
let numbers = [1, 2, 3, 4];
let sum = numbers.reduce(function(acc, num) {
    return acc + num;
}, 0); // Initial value is 0
console.log(sum); // Output: 10
```

Multi-dimensional Arrays

A multi-dimensional array is an array that contains other arrays as its elements. These are often referred to as "arrays of arrays."

- **Example** (2D array):

  javascript

  ```
  let matrix = [
      [1, 2, 3],
      [4, 5, 6],
      [7, 8, 9]
  ];
  console.log(matrix[0][0]); // Output: 1 (first element of the first sub-array)
  console.log(matrix[2][1]); // Output: 8 (second element of the third sub-array)
  ```

- **Iterating through multi-dimensional arrays**: You can use nested loops to iterate through multi-dimensional arrays.

  Example:

  javascript

  ```
  let matrix = [
      [1, 2, 3],
      [4, 5, 6],
  ```

```
    [7, 8, 9]
];
for (let i = 0; i < matrix.length; i++) {
    for (let j = 0; j < matrix[i].length; j++) {
        console.log(matrix[i][j]);
    }
}
// Output: 1 2 3 4 5 6 7 8 9
```

In this chapter, you've learned how to create and manipulate arrays in JavaScript. You've explored methods like push(), pop(), shift(), and unshift(), and you've worked with more advanced methods such as slice(), splice(), map(), filter(), and reduce(). Additionally, you've learned how to work with **multi-dimensional arrays**, which are essential when dealing with complex data structures. Understanding these array methods will help you perform powerful and efficient operations on data in your applications.

Chapter 7: Objects and Object-Oriented JavaScript

In JavaScript, **objects** are the most important data structure for storing and managing collections of data. They represent real-world entities and are essential for object-oriented programming (OOP). This chapter explores how to create and work with objects, how to define object properties and methods, and how JavaScript's **object-oriented programming** features like constructors, the this keyword, prototypes, and inheritance work.

Creating and Working with Objects

Objects are created in JavaScript using either the **object literal syntax** or the **Object constructor**.

1. **Object Literal Syntax**: The object literal is the simplest and most common way to create an object. It uses curly braces {} and key-value pairs where the key (or property) is a string, and the value can be any valid JavaScript data type.

   Example:

   javascript

```
let person = {
    name: "John",
    age: 30,
    greet: function() {
        console.log("Hello, " + this.name);
    }
};
```

```
console.log(person.name); // Output: John
console.log(person.age);  // Output: 30
person.greet();         // Output: Hello, John
```

In this example:

- o   name and age are properties of the object person.
- o   greet is a method (a function stored as a property of the object) that logs a greeting using the name property.

2. **Object Constructor**: Another way to create an object is by using the Object constructor, though this method is less commonly used compared to the literal syntax.

Example:

javascript

```
let person = new Object();
person.name = "John";
person.age = 30;
person.greet = function() {
```

```
    console.log("Hello, " + this.name);
};
```

```
console.log(person.name); // Output: John
console.log(person.age);  // Output: 30
person.greet();          // Output: Hello, John
```

Object Properties and Methods

1. **Object Properties**: Properties are values associated with an object, which can be any valid JavaScript data type, including numbers, strings, arrays, and even other objects.

   Example:

   javascript

   ```
   let car = {
      brand: "Toyota",
      model: "Camry",
      year: 2020
   };
   console.log(car.brand); // Output: Toyota
   console.log(car["model"]); // Output: Camry
   ```

   o You can access object properties using either dot notation (car.brand) or bracket notation (car["model"]).

2. **Object Methods**: Methods are functions that are stored as properties within an object. You can define methods to

perform operations on the object's properties or any other logic related to the object.

Example:

javascript

```javascript
let person = {
    firstName: "Alice",
    lastName: "Johnson",
    fullName: function() {
        return this.firstName + " " + this.lastName;
    }
};
console.log(person.fullName()); // Output: Alice Johnson
```

Object Constructor and this Keyword

1. **Object Constructor**: An **object constructor** is a function used to create new objects of a specific type. It works like a blueprint for creating objects with similar properties and methods.

Example:

javascript

```javascript
function Person(name, age) {
    this.name = name;
```

```
    this.age = age;
    this.greet = function() {
        console.log("Hello, " + this.name);
    };
}


let person1 = new Person("John", 30);
let person2 = new Person("Alice", 25);


console.log(person1.name);  // Output: John
console.log(person2.age);   // Output: 25
person1.greet();            // Output: Hello, John
```

- o   Person is an object constructor, and the new keyword creates a new object of the Person type.
- o   this refers to the object that the constructor is currently creating (person1 and person2 in the example).

2. **this Keyword**: The this keyword refers to the object that is executing the current function. It is used inside methods to access the object's properties and methods.

Example:

javascript

```
let person = {
    firstName: "Bob",
    lastName: "Smith",
    fullName: function() {
```

```javascript
    return this.firstName + " " + this.lastName;
  }
};
```

```javascript
console.log(person.fullName()); // Output: Bob Smith
```

   o   Inside the fullName() method, this.firstName refers to the firstName property of the person object.

Prototypes and Inheritance

JavaScript uses **prototype-based inheritance**, where objects can inherit properties and methods from other objects. Every JavaScript object has a **prototype**, which is another object from which it can inherit properties and methods.

1. **Prototypes**: The prototype is an object that provides shared properties and methods for other objects. If a property or method is not found in the object itself, JavaScript will look for it in the object's prototype.

   Example:

   javascript

   ```javascript
   function Person(name, age) {
       this.name = name;
       this.age = age;
   ```

```
}
```

```
Person.prototype.greet = function() {
    console.log("Hello, " + this.name);
};
```

```
let person1 = new Person("John", 30);
person1.greet(); // Output: Hello, John
```

- o In this example, the greet method is not defined inside the Person constructor, but instead, it is added to the Person prototype.
- o All instances of Person will inherit the greet method from the Person.prototype.

2. **Inheritance**: JavaScript supports inheritance through prototypes, meaning an object can inherit properties and methods from another object.

Example:

javascript

```
function Animal(name) {
    this.name = name;
}
```

```
Animal.prototype.speak = function() {
    console.log(this.name + " makes a sound");
};
```

```
function Dog(name, breed) {
    Animal.call(this, name);  // Inherit properties from Animal
    this.breed = breed;
}


// Inherit methods from Animal
Dog.prototype = Object.create(Animal.prototype);


Dog.prototype.bark = function() {
    console.log(this.name + " barks");
};


let dog1 = new Dog("Rex", "Labrador");
dog1.speak();  // Output: Rex makes a sound
dog1.bark();   // Output: Rex barks
```

- o The Dog constructor inherits properties from the Animal constructor using Animal.call(this, name).

- o The Dog prototype is set to inherit from Animal.prototype, so dog1 can call speak() and bark() methods.

- o This demonstrates **classical inheritance** in JavaScript through prototypes.

3. **Object.create()**: The Object.create() method is used to create a new object with the specified prototype object. This is a more modern and explicit way to set up inheritance.

Example:

javascript

```
let animal = {
   speak: function() {
      console.log(this.name + " makes a sound");
   }
};


let dog = Object.create(animal);
dog.name = "Buddy";
dog.speak(); // Output: Buddy makes a sound
```

- o In this example, dog is created with animal as its prototype, meaning dog inherits the speak() method from animal.

In this chapter, you've learned how to create and manipulate objects in JavaScript. You explored object properties and methods, how to use the this keyword, and how to create objects using constructors. You also studied the concepts of **prototypes** and **inheritance**, which allow you to create objects that can inherit properties and methods from other objects. These object-oriented concepts are powerful tools for organizing and managing complex code and are essential for mastering JavaScript.

Chapter 8: Event Handling and DOM Manipulation

In JavaScript, interaction with a webpage is facilitated through the **Document Object Model (DOM)**, which represents the structure of an HTML document as a tree of objects. This chapter explores how to interact with the DOM, handle events, and manipulate the content of a webpage dynamically using JavaScript.

Introduction to the Document Object Model (DOM)

The **DOM** is an interface that allows JavaScript to manipulate the structure, style, and content of an HTML document. It represents the entire HTML document as a tree of nodes, where each node corresponds to part of the document (e.g., elements, attributes, and text).

- **DOM Tree Structure**: The document is represented as a tree where the topmost node is the document, and every element (like <div>, <p>, <button>, etc.) is represented as a node in the tree.

  Example:

html

```
<html>
  <head><title>Page Title</title></head>
  <body>
    <h1>Heading</h1>
    <p>Paragraph content here.</p>
    <button id="myButton">Click Me!</button>
  </body>
</html>
```

In the DOM, the document node contains all the HTML elements (head, body, etc.), and each element is a node in the tree.

Accessing DOM Elements Using JavaScript

JavaScript allows you to interact with the DOM and manipulate elements by accessing them using various methods.

1. **getElementById()**: This method is used to access an element by its unique id attribute.

Example:

javascript

```
let button = document.getElementById("myButton");
console.log(button);    // Output: <button id="myButton">Click Me!</button>
```

2. **getElementsByClassName()**: This method returns a collection of all elements with a specified class name.

   Example:

   javascript

   ```
   let paragraphs = document.getElementsByClassName("paragraph");
   console.log(paragraphs);  // Output: HTMLCollection of elements with class "paragraph"
   ```

3. **getElementsByTagName()**: This method returns a collection of all elements with a specified tag name.

   Example:

   javascript

   ```
   let divs = document.getElementsByTagName("div");
   console.log(divs); // Output: HTMLCollection of <div> elements
   ```

4. **querySelector()**: The querySelector() method returns the first element that matches a specified CSS selector.

   Example:

   javascript

   ```
   let firstParagraph = document.querySelector("p");
   console.log(firstParagraph); // Output: <p>Paragraph content here.</p>
   ```

5. **querySelectorAll()**: The querySelectorAll() method returns a **NodeList** of all elements matching a specified CSS selector.

Example:

javascript

```
let allParagraphs = document.querySelectorAll("p");
console.log(allParagraphs);  // Output: NodeList of all <p> elements
```

Event Handling: addEventListener, Event Object, Event Propagation

Event handling allows you to respond to user actions, such as clicks, key presses, mouse movements, etc. JavaScript provides the addEventListener() method to attach event handlers to elements.

1. **addEventListener()**: The addEventListener() method is used to bind an event handler to an element. It listens for a specific event and calls a function when that event occurs.

Syntax:

javascript

```
element.addEventListener(event, function, useCapture);
```

  o event: The name of the event to listen for (e.g., click, mouseover, keydown).

o function: The function that will be executed when the event is triggered.

o useCapture (optional): A Boolean value that determines whether the event should be captured during the capturing phase (default is false).

Example:

javascript

```javascript
let button = document.getElementById("myButton");
button.addEventListener("click", function() {
    alert("Button clicked!");
});
```

In this example, when the button is clicked, an alert will be displayed with the message "Button clicked!".

2. **Event Object**: The event object is automatically passed to the event handler function and contains useful information about the event, such as the type of event, the target element, and mouse position.

Example:

javascript

```javascript
let button = document.getElementById("myButton");
button.addEventListener("click", function(event) {
    console.log("Event type: " + event.type); // Output: Event type: click
```

```
    console.log("Event target: " + event.target);   // Output: <button
id="myButton">Click Me!</button>
});
```

The event object provides details about the event, such as the element that triggered the event (event.target) and the type of event (event.type).

3. **Event Propagation (Bubbling and Capturing)**: JavaScript events can propagate through the DOM in two phases: **capturing** and **bubbling**.

    o   **Event Capturing**: The event is first captured by the outermost element and propagated down to the target element.

    o   **Event Bubbling**: The event bubbles up from the target element to the outer elements (default behavior).

    Example of Bubbling:

    html

```
<div id="outerDiv">
   <button id="innerButton">Click Me!</button>
</div>

<script>
   document.getElementById("outerDiv").addEventListener("click",
function() {
```

```
    console.log("Outer div clicked!");
  });


  document.getElementById("innerButton").addEventListener("click",
function(event) {
    console.log("Button clicked!");
    event.stopPropagation();  // Stops the event from bubbling
  });
</script>
```
Output:

- o If event.stopPropagation() is not used, clicking the button will trigger both the button's and the outer div's event listeners.
- o If event.stopPropagation() is used, the event will not bubble up to the outerDiv, and only the button's event handler will be executed.

Modifying the DOM (Changing Text, Styles, Attributes)

JavaScript allows you to modify the content and appearance of the webpage by manipulating the DOM elements. You can change text, styles, and attributes dynamically.

1. **Changing Text**: You can modify the text content of an element using the textContent or innerText properties.

Example:

javascript

```
let heading = document.querySelector("h1");
heading.textContent = "New Heading Text";
```

2. **Changing HTML Content**: You can modify the HTML content of an element using the innerHTML property.

Example:

javascript

```
let paragraph = document.querySelector("p");
paragraph.innerHTML = "This is <strong>bold</strong> text!";
```

   o   In this example, the innerHTML property is used to insert HTML tags, such as <strong>, into the element.

3. **Changing Styles**: You can modify the styles of an element using the style property.

Example:

javascript

```
let paragraph = document.querySelector("p");
paragraph.style.color = "red";
paragraph.style.fontSize = "20px";
```

    o   In this example, the color of the text is changed to red, and the font size is set to 20px.

4. **Changing Attributes**: You can modify the attributes of an element, such as src for images or href for links, using the setAttribute() method.

Example:

javascript

```
let image = document.querySelector("img");
image.setAttribute("src", "new-image.jpg");
image.setAttribute("alt", "New image description");
```

5. **Adding/Removing Classes**: You can add or remove classes from elements to change their appearance dynamically using the classList API.

    o   **add()**: Adds a class to an element.

    o   **remove()**: Removes a class from an element.

Example:

javascript

```
let button = document.querySelector("button");
button.classList.add("active");
button.classList.remove("inactive");
```

In this chapter, you learned how to interact with the **DOM** using JavaScript, how to **access elements** using various methods, and how to **handle events** using addEventListener(). You also explored **event propagation** and the event object. Finally, you learned how to **modify the DOM** by changing text, styles, attributes, and adding/removing classes. Mastering these techniques is essential for creating interactive and dynamic web applications with JavaScript.

Chapter 9: Error Handling and Debugging

Error handling and debugging are crucial skills for every JavaScript developer. Even experienced developers make mistakes in their code, and understanding how to effectively handle and fix errors is essential for building robust applications. In this chapter, we'll explore the different types of errors in JavaScript, how to handle them using try...catch, and how to utilize browser tools and common techniques to debug your code.

Types of Errors: Syntax, Runtime, Logic Errors

Errors in JavaScript generally fall into three categories: **syntax errors**, **runtime errors**, and **logic errors**. Each type of error requires a different approach to handle and fix.

1. **Syntax Errors**: A syntax error occurs when the JavaScript code is not written correctly according to the language's syntax rules. These errors are usually detected when the code is parsed, and they prevent the script from running.

   Example:

javascript

```
let name = "John';  // Syntax error: missing closing quote
```

- o In this example, the string is missing the closing quote, causing a syntax error.

Fix:

javascript

```
let name = "John";  // Corrected syntax
```

2. **Runtime Errors**: A runtime error occurs while the code is running. These errors happen when the program attempts an operation that is impossible or invalid during execution.

Example:

javascript

```
let num = 10;
console.log(num.toUpperCase());  // Runtime error: num is a number, not a string
```

- o In this example, trying to call toUpperCase() on a number results in a runtime error.

Fix:

javascript

```javascript
let num = "10";
console.log(num.toUpperCase()); // Corrected: num is now a string
```

3. **Logic Errors**: A logic error occurs when the code runs without any syntax or runtime issues, but it does not behave as expected. These errors are more difficult to detect because the program does not crash; instead, it produces incorrect output.

   Example:

   javascript

   ```javascript
   function add(a, b) {
       return a - b; // Logic error: subtraction instead of addition
   }
   console.log(add(5, 3)); // Output: 2 (Expected: 8)
   ```

   Fix:

   javascript

   ```javascript
   function add(a, b) {
       return a + b; // Corrected logic
   }
   console.log(add(5, 3)); // Output: 8
   ```

Using try...catch to Handle Errors

JavaScript provides the try...catch statement to handle runtime errors gracefully. The code inside the try block is executed, and if an error occurs, the control is transferred to the catch block, where the error can be handled or logged.

1. **Basic Syntax**:

javascript

```
try {
    // Code that may cause an error
} catch (error) {
    // Code that runs if an error occurs
}
```

2. **Example of try...catch**:

javascript

```
try {
    let result = 10 / 0;  // No error, but this results in Infinity
    console.log(result);
} catch (error) {
    console.log("An error occurred: " + error.message);
}
```

   o   The catch block will catch any errors that occur within the try block. In this case, even though dividing by 0 doesn't throw an exception, it would produce Infinity, which can still be handled in the catch block if you wish to handle or log such results explicitly.

3. **Throwing Custom Errors**: You can throw your own errors using the throw statement. This is useful for enforcing rules or constraints within your code.

Example:

javascript

```
try {
    let age = -5;
    if (age < 0) {
        throw new Error("Age cannot be negative");
    }
} catch (error) {
    console.log(error.message);  // Output: Age cannot be negative
}
```

o In this example, a custom error is thrown if the age is negative.

Debugging Tools in Browsers

Modern browsers provide built-in developer tools to help you debug your JavaScript code. These tools allow you to inspect the DOM, track network requests, and use a JavaScript console to log messages, view errors, and interact with your code.

1. **Console**: The console is the most basic debugging tool, allowing you to print messages and errors in your code.

   o Use console.log() to output values or messages to the console.

   o Use console.error() to display error messages.

   o Use console.warn() to display warnings.

   o Example:

   javascript

   ```javascript
   console.log("This is a log message");
   console.error("This is an error message");
   console.warn("This is a warning message");
   ```

2. **Browser Developer Tools**: Every major browser (Chrome, Firefox, Safari, Edge) includes developer tools that allow you to inspect and debug JavaScript code. To open these tools, you can typically press **F12** or **Ctrl+Shift+I**.

   Key features include:

   o **Sources Tab**: View, edit, and set breakpoints in your JavaScript files.

   o **Console Tab**: View log messages, errors, and warnings.

   o **Network Tab**: Track API requests, monitor server communication, and inspect HTTP requests.

o **Elements Tab**: Inspect the DOM and see how JavaScript changes HTML content.

Example:

o Open the **Sources Tab** in Chrome and set a breakpoint by clicking on the line number in the JavaScript file. This will pause the execution of the code at that line, allowing you to inspect variables and the call stack.

3. **Breakpoints**: A **breakpoint** is a powerful tool for stopping code execution at a specific line, which allows you to inspect variables, step through your code, and identify the source of bugs.

   o **Setting a breakpoint**: In the **Sources Tab**, you can click on the line number where you want to stop the code. Once the breakpoint is set, running the code will pause execution at that line, allowing you to inspect the current state of the program.

Common Debugging Techniques

1. **Use console.log() for Tracing**: The simplest and most common debugging technique is adding console.log() statements in your code to output values and track the flow

of execution. This helps identify where the program is going wrong.

Example:

javascript

```
function add(a, b) {
    console.log("a: " + a, "b: " + b);  // Trace the values of a and b
    return a + b;
}
let result = add(5, "10");  // Output: a: 5 b: 10
console.log(result);  // Output: 510 (because of type coercion)
```

2. **Step Through Code Using Breakpoints**: As mentioned earlier, using breakpoints in the browser's developer tools allows you to pause the execution of your code and inspect variable values. You can step through each line of code to see how it behaves.

3. **Check for Undefined Variables**: Undefined variables are a common source of bugs. Use the console or debugger to check whether a variable has been initialized properly.

4. **Isolate the Issue**: Try to isolate the part of the code that is causing the error. You can comment out sections of the code and re-enable them one by one to narrow down the issue.

5. **Use Stack Traces**: When an error occurs, JavaScript usually provides a **stack trace** that shows the sequence of function

calls that led to the error. You can use the stack trace to trace the error back to its source.

Example:

javascript

```
try {
    let result = nonExistentFunction();
} catch (error) {
    console.log(error.stack);
}
```

o   This will print the stack trace to the console, which helps you trace the error back to the function that caused it.

In this chapter, you've learned about the **different types of errors** in JavaScript, including **syntax**, **runtime**, and **logic errors**. You've also explored how to handle errors using **try...catch** blocks and how to use **browser developer tools** for debugging. Finally, we discussed **common debugging techniques**, such as using console.log(), setting breakpoints, and checking variable states. Mastering these techniques is essential for effective problem-solving and writing error-free, reliable JavaScript code.

Chapter 10: Working with Strings

Strings are one of the most commonly used data types in JavaScript. They represent sequences of characters and come with a variety of methods to manipulate, transform, and search within text. This chapter covers key string methods, string interpolation, basic string manipulation techniques, and an introduction to regular expressions (regex) for working with more complex string patterns.

String Methods: length, indexOf, slice, substring

JavaScript provides a rich set of built-in methods for strings that allow you to perform various operations like finding lengths, extracting portions of a string, or searching for specific text.

1. **length**: The length property returns the number of characters in a string.

   Example:

   javascript

   ```
   let greeting = "Hello, world!";
   console.log(greeting.length); // Output: 13
   ```

2. **indexOf()**: The indexOf() method returns the index of the first occurrence of a specified value in a string. If the value is not found, it returns -1.

   Example:

   javascript

   ```
   let message = "Hello, world!";
   console.log(message.indexOf("world"));  // Output: 7
   console.log(message.indexOf("JavaScript"));  // Output: -1
   ```

3. **slice()**: The slice() method extracts a part of a string and returns it as a new string. It takes two arguments: the start index and the end index (optional).

   Example:

   javascript

   ```
   let text = "JavaScript is fun!";
   console.log(text.slice(0, 10));  // Output: JavaScript
   console.log(text.slice(11));  // Output: is fun!
   ```

   o The slice() method does not modify the original string; instead, it returns a new string.

4. **substring()**: The substring() method also extracts a part of a string between two indices, but it behaves slightly differently from slice() when negative indices are used.

Example:

javascript

```
let text = "JavaScript is fun!";
console.log(text.substring(0, 10));  // Output: JavaScript
console.log(text.substring(11, 14));  // Output: is
```

- o The key difference is that substring() will swap the start and end indices if they are provided in reverse order.

Template Literals and String Interpolation

Template literals, introduced in **ES6 (ECMAScript 2015)**, provide an easy way to embed expressions into strings. Template literals use backticks (`) instead of single or double quotes and allow you to embed variables and expressions inside the string.

1. **String Interpolation**: You can embed variables or expressions inside a string by using ${} syntax within a template literal.

   Example:

   javascript

   ```
   let name = "Alice";
   ```

```
let age = 25;
let greeting = `Hello, my name is ${name} and I am ${age} years old.`;
console.log(greeting);  // Output: Hello, my name is Alice and I am 25
years old.
```

2. **Multiline Strings**: Template literals can span multiple lines, making them easier to write and read compared to strings with explicit newline characters (\n).

   Example:

   javascript

   ```
   let message = `This is a
   multiline string
   using template literals.`;
   console.log(message);
   ```

   o The string automatically preserves newlines between the backticks.

String Manipulation Techniques

JavaScript provides several methods to manipulate strings, such as replacing parts of a string, trimming spaces, converting case, and more.

1. **toUpperCase() and toLowerCase()**: These methods convert a string to uppercase or lowercase, respectively.

   Example:

   javascript

   ```
   let message = "Hello, World!";
   console.log(message.toUpperCase());  // Output: HELLO, WORLD!
   console.log(message.toLowerCase());  // Output: hello, world!
   ```

2. **replace()**: The replace() method searches for a specified value or regular expression and replaces it with another value.

   Example:

   javascript

   ```
   let sentence = "JavaScript is great!";
   let newSentence = sentence.replace("great", "awesome");
   console.log(newSentence);  // Output: JavaScript is awesome!
   ```

   o The replace() method only replaces the first occurrence of the value. To replace all occurrences, use a global regular expression.

3. **trim()**: The trim() method removes whitespace from both ends of a string.

   Example:

javascript

```
let text = "   Hello, World!   ";
console.log(text.trim());  // Output: "Hello, World!"
```

4. **split()**: The split() method divides a string into an array of substrings based on a specified delimiter.

   Example:

   javascript

   ```
   let sentence = "JavaScript is awesome";
   let words = sentence.split(" ");
   console.log(words);  // Output: ["JavaScript", "is", "awesome"]
   ```

5. **charAt()**: The charAt() method returns the character at a specific index in a string.

   Example:

   javascript

   ```
   let text = "JavaScript";
   console.log(text.charAt(4));  // Output: S
   ```

6. **includes()**: The includes() method checks whether a string contains a specified substring and returns a boolean value (true or false).

Example:

javascript

```
let sentence = "JavaScript is fun!";
console.log(sentence.includes("fun"));  // Output: true
console.log(sentence.includes("Python"));  // Output: false
```

Regular Expressions Basics

Regular expressions (regex) are patterns used to match character combinations in strings. They provide a powerful way to search, validate, and manipulate text. In JavaScript, regular expressions are created using two methods: regex literals and the RegExp constructor.

1. **Creating Regular Expressions**: You can define a regular expression either using regex literals or the RegExp constructor.

   o **Regex Literal**:

   javascript

   ```
   let regex = /hello/;
   ```

   o **RegExp Constructor**:

   javascript

   ```
   let regex = new RegExp("hello");
   ```

2. **Basic Regex Patterns**: Regular expressions allow you to define search patterns for matching specific text.

   o **. (dot)**: Matches any single character except newline characters.

   o **^**: Matches the beginning of a string.

   o **$**: Matches the end of a string.

   o **[abc]**: Matches any character a, b, or c.

   o **\d**: Matches any digit (0-9).

   o **\w**: Matches any word character (alphanumeric plus underscore).

Example:

javascript

```
let regex = /\d+/;  // Matches one or more digits
let result = "There are 100 apples".match(regex);
console.log(result);  // Output: ["100"]
```

3. **Testing Strings**: The test() method tests whether a string matches a regular expression and returns true or false.

Example:

javascript

```
let regex = /hello/;
console.log(regex.test("hello world"));  // Output: true
console.log(regex.test("hi world"));  // Output: false
```

4. **Replacing Text with Regular Expressions**: The replace() method can also accept a regular expression to replace matching text.

   Example:

   javascript

   ```
   let sentence = "JavaScript is awesome!";
   let newSentence = sentence.replace(/awesome/, "amazing");
   console.log(newSentence);  // Output: JavaScript is amazing!
   ```

5. **Global and Case-Insensitive Flags**: You can use flags in regular expressions to perform global searches or make searches case-insensitive.
   - **g**: Global search (match all occurrences).
   - **i**: Case-insensitive search.

   Example:

   javascript

   ```
   let sentence = "JavaScript is great. I love JavaScript!";
   let regex = /javascript/gi;  // Global and case-insensitive search
   let result = sentence.replace(regex, "awesome");
   console.log(result);  // Output: awesome is great. I love awesome!
   ```

In this chapter, you've learned how to work with strings in JavaScript, from basic string methods like length, indexOf, slice, and substring, to advanced concepts like **template literals**, **string manipulation techniques**, and **regular expressions**. Mastering these string operations allows you to efficiently process and manipulate text, which is a vital part of building dynamic and responsive applications in JavaScript.

Chapter 11: JavaScript and the Web: Making Requests

In modern web development, interacting with remote servers is an essential task. JavaScript provides several ways to make HTTP requests, retrieve data from servers, and handle responses. This chapter covers the use of **XMLHttpRequest**, the more modern **Fetch API**, making **GET** and **POST** requests, and working with **JSON** data, which is commonly used for communication between a web client and a server.

The XMLHttpRequest Object

The **XMLHttpRequest (XHR)** object is an older API that allows JavaScript to send HTTP requests to a web server and receive responses. Although newer APIs like fetch() are preferred, understanding XMLHttpRequest is still useful because of its widespread use in older applications.

1. **Creating an XMLHttpRequest**: To use the XMLHttpRequest object, you first need to create a new instance.

   Example:

javascript

```
let xhr = new XMLHttpRequest();
```

2. **Opening a Request**: After creating the request object, you must configure it by specifying the HTTP method (GET, POST, etc.) and the URL to which the request should be sent.

Syntax:

javascript

```
xhr.open(method, url, async);
```

- o method: The HTTP method (e.g., "GET", "POST").
- o url: The URL to which the request is sent.
- o async: A boolean indicating whether the request should be asynchronous (true) or synchronous (false).

Example:

javascript

```
xhr.open("GET", "https://jsonplaceholder.typicode.com/posts", true);
```

3. **Sending the Request**: Once the request is opened, you can send it using the send() method. For GET requests, you don't need to pass any parameters, but for POST requests, you can send data with the request.

Example:

javascript

xhr.send();

4. **Handling the Response**: You can use the onload event handler to process the response when the request completes. The responseText property contains the raw response data.

Example:

javascript

```
xhr.onload = function() {
    if (xhr.status === 200) {
        console.log(xhr.responseText);  // Output: Response data from the
server
    } else {
        console.error("Request failed with status: " + xhr.status);
    }
};
```

- o xhr.status: Contains the HTTP status code of the response (200 indicates success).
- o xhr.responseText: Contains the response data as a string.

Introduction to Fetch API

The **Fetch API** is a modern, promise-based API that provides a more flexible and powerful way to make HTTP requests. It is a more readable and easier-to-use alternative to XMLHttpRequest.

1. **Basic Syntax**: The fetch() function is used to make HTTP requests and returns a **Promise** that resolves with the response.

   Syntax:

   javascript

   ```javascript
   fetch(url, options)
       .then(response => response.json())
       .then(data => console.log(data))
       .catch(error => console.error('Error:', error));
   ```

   o url: The URL to which the request is sent.

   o options (optional): An object containing additional settings (e.g., HTTP method, headers, body).

   o response.json(): A method that converts the response to a JSON object.

2. **Making a GET Request**: The simplest form of using fetch() is making a GET request, which retrieves data from a server.

   Example:

   javascript

```
fetch("https://jsonplaceholder.typicode.com/posts")
  .then(response => response.json()) // Parse JSON data
  .then(data => console.log(data))   // Log the data
  .catch(error => console.error("Error:", error));
```

- o The response.json() method parses the response body as JSON, which is a common format used by APIs.

3. **Making a POST Request**: A POST request is used to send data to the server, such as submitting form data or creating a new resource.

Example:

javascript

```
fetch("https://jsonplaceholder.typicode.com/posts", {
  method: "POST",
  headers: {
    "Content-Type": "application/json"
  },
  body: JSON.stringify({
    title: "foo",
    body: "bar",
    userId: 1
  })
})
  .then(response => response.json())
  .then(data => console.log(data))
  .catch(error => console.error("Error:", error));
```

o The method: "POST" option specifies that the request will be a POST request.

o The body option contains the data to be sent, and it must be stringified if it's an object (e.g., using JSON.stringify()).

o The headers option sets the Content-Type to application/json to indicate that the request body contains JSON data.

Making GET and POST Requests

Making GET and POST requests is a common pattern in client-server communication. Let's look at both in more detail.

1. **GET Request**: GET requests are used to retrieve data from a server. You typically use GET requests to fetch data from APIs.

Example:

javascript

```
fetch("https://jsonplaceholder.typicode.com/posts")
    .then(response => response.json())
    .then(data => console.log(data))
    .catch(error => console.error("Error:", error));
```

o **GET requests** do not include a body, and the data is often retrieved in the URL query parameters or as part of the URL path.

2. **POST Request**: POST requests are used to send data to the server, typically to create or update resources. You can send data in the request body.

Example:

javascript

```
fetch("https://jsonplaceholder.typicode.com/posts", {
    method: "POST",
    headers: {
        "Content-Type": "application/json"
    },
    body: JSON.stringify({
        title: "foo",
        body: "bar",
        userId: 1
    })
})
.then(response => response.json())
.then(data => console.log(data))
.catch(error => console.error("Error:", error));
```

o The body option contains the data to be sent to the server.

o The headers option defines the type of content being sent (in this case, JSON).

Working with JSON Data

JSON (JavaScript Object Notation) is the most commonly used format for data exchange between a server and a client. JavaScript provides built-in methods to parse and stringify JSON data.

1. **Parsing JSON**: When receiving JSON data from the server (as a response), you need to parse it into a JavaScript object. You can do this with response.json() in the Fetch API.

   Example:

   javascript

   ```javascript
   fetch("https://jsonplaceholder.typicode.com/posts")
       .then(response => response.json()) // Parse the JSON response
       .then(data => {
         console.log(data);
   })
   .catch(error => console.error("Error:", error));
   ```

   o The response.json() method converts the response body from a JSON string into a JavaScript object.

2. **Stringifying JSON**: When sending data to a server (e.g., in a POST request), you need to convert a JavaScript object into a JSON string. You can do this with JSON.stringify().

Example:

javascript

```
let data = {
    title: "foo",
    body: "bar",
    userId: 1
};

fetch("https://jsonplaceholder.typicode.com/posts", {
    method: "POST",
    headers: {
        "Content-Type": "application/json"
    },
    body: JSON.stringify(data)  // Convert the object to a JSON string
})
.then(response => response.json())
.then(result => console.log(result))
.catch(error => console.error("Error:", error));
```

o   JSON.stringify() converts the JavaScript object data into a JSON string suitable for transmission over HTTP.

In this chapter, you've learned how to interact with the web in JavaScript using **XMLHttpRequest** and the modern **Fetch API**. You've seen how to make **GET** and **POST** requests, and how to work with **JSON** data, which is essential for client-server communication. Understanding these techniques is fundamental for building dynamic web applications that can retrieve, send, and manipulate data from external servers.

Chapter 12: Asynchronous JavaScript: Callbacks and Promises

Asynchronous programming is essential for handling tasks that take time to complete, such as making HTTP requests, reading files, or processing large amounts of data. JavaScript, by default, runs synchronously, meaning each line of code is executed one after the other. However, asynchronous operations allow us to execute tasks in the background without blocking the rest of the code, improving the performance and responsiveness of web applications. In this chapter, we'll explore **callbacks**, **Promises**, and how to manage asynchronous operations efficiently.

Understanding Asynchronous Programming

Asynchronous programming allows JavaScript to perform tasks like I/O operations (e.g., reading files, fetching data from APIs) without blocking the execution of the rest of the code.

- **Synchronous programming** executes tasks one after another, meaning each task waits for the previous one to complete before starting.

- **Asynchronous programming** allows tasks to start and run independently, with JavaScript being able to handle other operations while waiting for the task to complete.

Example of Synchronous Code:

javascript

```
console.log("First task");
console.log("Second task");
console.log("Third task");
```

- Output:

  sql

  First task
  Second task
  Third task

Example of Asynchronous Code (with a delay):

javascript

```
console.log("First task");

setTimeout(function() {
    console.log("Second task");
}, 1000);

console.log("Third task");
```

- Output:

sql

First task
Third task
Second task (after 1 second delay)

In this example, the setTimeout function delays the execution of the second task for 1 second, allowing the third task to execute immediately after the first task.

Using Callbacks in JavaScript

A **callback** is a function that is passed into another function as an argument and is executed after the completion of that function. In asynchronous programming, callbacks are used to handle the result of an asynchronous operation.

1. **Basic Callback Example**: In the example below, the processUserData function takes two arguments: user data and a callback function that is executed after the data is processed.

   Example:

   javascript

   ```
   function fetchData(callback) {
       let data = "User data";
   ```

```
  console.log("Fetching data...");
  callback(data);
}
```

```
function processData(data) {
  console.log("Processing: " + data);
}
```

```
fetchData(processData);   // Output: Fetching data... Processing: User
data
```

2. **Asynchronous Callback Example**: A common use of callbacks in JavaScript is when working with asynchronous functions such as setTimeout, fetch, or file reading.

   Example:

   javascript

   ```
   console.log("Starting process...");
   ```

   ```
   setTimeout(function() {
     console.log("Data fetched from server");
   }, 2000);
   ```

   ```
   console.log("Process finished!");
   ```

   o The setTimeout function simulates fetching data from a server. Even though the setTimeout is asynchronous,

JavaScript continues executing the rest of the code without waiting for the 2-second delay to complete.

Introduction to Promises

A **Promise** is a more modern and flexible way of handling asynchronous operations compared to callbacks. A Promise represents the eventual completion (or failure) of an asynchronous operation and its resulting value. It has three states:

- **Pending**: The operation is still in progress.
- **Resolved (Fulfilled)**: The operation completed successfully, and the promise is now settled.
- **Rejected**: The operation failed, and the promise is settled with an error.

1. **Creating a Promise**: You can create a Promise using the new Promise() constructor. This constructor takes a function with two arguments: resolve and reject.

   Example:

   javascript

   ```
   let promise = new Promise(function(resolve, reject) {
       let success = true;
       if (success) {
   ```

```
      resolve("Operation successful!");
    } else {
      reject("Operation failed.");
    }
});
```

```
promise.then(function(value) {
    console.log(value);  // Output: Operation successful!
}).catch(function(error) {
    console.error(error);
});
```

- o resolve() is called when the promise is successful.

- o reject() is called when the promise fails.

2. **Promise Lifecycle**: A promise starts in the **pending** state, then moves to **resolved** if the operation succeeds, or **rejected** if it fails. You can attach .then() and .catch() handlers to handle the outcome.

Example:

javascript

```
let promise = new Promise((resolve, reject) => {
    let success = true;
    if (success) {
      resolve("Data successfully fetched!");
    } else {
      reject("Error fetching data.");
    }
```

```
});
```

promise

```
.then(result => console.log(result))   // Output: Data successfully
fetched!
    .catch(error => console.log(error)); // Output: Error fetching data. (if
failure occurs)
```

Chaining Promises and Handling Errors

Promise chaining allows you to run multiple asynchronous operations one after another, ensuring that each operation happens only after the previous one completes.

1. **Chaining Promises**: You can chain multiple .then() handlers to execute a sequence of asynchronous operations.

    Example:

    javascript

```
let promise = new Promise((resolve, reject) => {
    let success = true;
    if (success) {
        resolve("Step 1 completed");
    } else {
        reject("Step 1 failed");
    }
});
```

```javascript
promise
  .then(result => {
    console.log(result);  // Output: Step 1 completed
    return "Step 2 completed";  // Returning a new value to the next
`.then()`
  })
  .then(result => {
    console.log(result);  // Output: Step 2 completed
  })
  .catch(error => {
    console.error("Error: " + error);
  });
```

- o Each .then() handler returns a new value, which can be passed to the next .then(). If an error occurs in any of the then blocks, it is passed to the .catch() block for error handling.

2. **Handling Errors in Promises**: Error handling in promises can be done using the .catch() method. If an error occurs at any point in the chain, the control will be passed to the .catch() method.

Example:

javascript

```javascript
let promise = new Promise((resolve, reject) => {
  let success = false;
  if (success) {
```

```
    resolve("Operation succeeded");
  } else {
    reject("Operation failed");
  }
});
```

```
promise
  .then(result => console.log(result))
  .catch(error => console.log("Error: " + error));  // Output: Error:
Operation failed
```

Handling Multiple Promises (Promise.all)

When dealing with multiple asynchronous operations, you can use Promise.all() to wait for all promises to resolve before proceeding with further logic.

1. **Promise.all()**: The Promise.all() method takes an array of promises and returns a new promise. It resolves when all promises in the array have resolved, or it rejects if any of the promises are rejected.

Example:

javascript

```
let promise1 = new Promise((resolve, reject) => resolve("Data 1"));
let promise2 = new Promise((resolve, reject) => resolve("Data 2"));
let promise3 = new Promise((resolve, reject) => resolve("Data 3"));
```

```
Promise.all([promise1, promise2, promise3])
  .then(results => {
    console.log(results);  // Output: ["Data 1", "Data 2", "Data 3"]
  })
  .catch(error => {
    console.log("Error:", error);
  });
```

- o If any of the promises are rejected, the catch() block will execute, and no further promises will be resolved.

In this chapter, you learned about **asynchronous programming** in JavaScript and how it enables non-blocking operations. You explored the **callback** pattern, the more modern **Promise** pattern for handling asynchronous operations, and how to chain multiple promises and handle errors effectively. Promises provide a cleaner and more manageable way to handle asynchronous tasks compared to callbacks, and they're essential for creating efficient, responsive applications in JavaScript.

Chapter 13: JavaScript ES6 Features

ECMAScript 6 (also known as **ES6** or **ECMAScript 2015**) brought many powerful features and improvements to JavaScript, making it more expressive, flexible, and efficient. These features have become standard in modern JavaScript development. In this chapter, we'll explore some of the key ES6 features, including let and const, **destructuring assignments**, **template literals**, **default parameters**, and the **rest/spread operators**.

Introduction to ES6 (ECMAScript 2015) Features
ES6 introduced many new features to JavaScript, improving both the language's syntax and capabilities. Some of the most important features include:

- Block-scoped variable declarations (let, const)
- Arrow functions
- Template literals
- Destructuring assignments
- Default parameters
- Rest and spread operators
- Classes and modules
- Promises

- Enhanced object literals

These features make JavaScript more concise and easier to work with, especially for complex applications.

Let and Const vs. Var

Before ES6, JavaScript only had the var keyword to declare variables. However, var has some scoping and hoisting issues that can lead to bugs. ES6 introduced let and const to address these problems.

1. let:

   o let allows you to declare variables with **block scope**, which means the variable is only accessible within the block (e.g., inside a loop or if statement).

   o let does not have the **hoisting** issues of var (variables declared with let are not accessible before their declaration).

Example:

javascript

```
let x = 10;
if (true) {
    let x = 20;  // This x is scoped to the if block
    console.log(x);  // Output: 20
}
```

console.log(x); // Output: 10

2. **const**:

   o const is used to declare **constant** variables whose values cannot be reassigned.

   o Like let, const is also block-scoped.

   o const is ideal for defining values that should not change.

Example:

javascript

const pi = 3.14;
// pi = 3.14159; // Error: Assignment to constant variable.

   o Note that while const prevents reassignment of the variable itself, it does not make objects or arrays immutable. The contents of a const object or array can still be modified.

Destructuring Assignments

Destructuring assignments allow you to unpack values from arrays or properties from objects into distinct variables, making the code cleaner and more readable.

1. **Array Destructuring**: You can extract values from arrays and assign them to variables in a concise manner.

   Example:

   javascript

   ```javascript
   const colors = ["red", "green", "blue"];
   const [first, second, third] = colors;
   console.log(first);  // Output: red
   console.log(second); // Output: green
   console.log(third);  // Output: blue
   ```

   o You can also skip values using commas:

   javascript

   ```javascript
   const colors = ["red", "green", "blue"];
   const [, second] = colors;
   console.log(second);  // Output: green
   ```

2. **Object Destructuring**: You can extract properties from objects and assign them to variables.

   Example:

   javascript

   ```javascript
   const person = { name: "Alice", age: 25, city: "New York" };
   const { name, age } = person;
   console.log(name); // Output: Alice
   ```

```
console.log(age);   // Output: 25
```

    o   You can also assign different names to the variables:

javascript

```
const person = { name: "Alice", age: 25 };
const { name: fullName, age: yearsOld } = person;
console.log(fullName);  // Output: Alice
console.log(yearsOld);  // Output: 25
```

Template Literals, Default Parameters, and Rest/Spread Operators

1. **Template Literals**: Template literals allow you to embed expressions inside strings using the ${} syntax. This makes string interpolation easier and allows for multi-line strings.

   o **String Interpolation**: You can insert variables or expressions inside the string.

Example:

javascript

```
let name = "Alice";
let greeting = `Hello, ${name}! How are you today?`;
console.log(greeting);  // Output: Hello, Alice! How are you today?
```

o **Multi-line Strings**: Template literals preserve line breaks and indentation.

Example:

javascript

```
let message = `
This is a
multi-line string
in JavaScript.`;
console.log(message);
```

2. **Default Parameters**: Default parameters allow you to assign default values to function parameters if no value is provided.

Example:

javascript

```
function greet(name = "Guest") {
    console.log(`Hello, ${name}!`);
}

greet();        // Output: Hello, Guest!
greet("Alice"); // Output: Hello, Alice!
```

    o   In this example, the name parameter has a default value of "Guest". If no argument is passed, the function uses the default value.

3. **Rest Operator**: The rest operator (...) allows you to gather multiple function arguments into an array. It is typically used for functions that take a variable number of arguments.

Example:

javascript

```
function sum(...numbers) {
    return numbers.reduce((acc, num) => acc + num, 0);
}

console.log(sum(1, 2, 3, 4)); // Output: 10
```

    o   The ...numbers syntax collects all arguments into an array, making it easier to work with a variable number of arguments.

4. **Spread Operator**: The spread operator (...) is used to unpack elements of an array or object into individual elements or properties. It is often used when ing arrays or combining objects.

    o   **Array Example**:

        javascript

```
const arr1 = [1, 2, 3];
const arr2 = [...arr1, 4, 5];
console.log(arr2);  // Output: [1, 2, 3, 4, 5]
```

o **Object Example**:

javascript

```
const person = { name: "Alice", age: 25 };
const updatedPerson = { ...person, city: "New York" };
console.log(updatedPerson);  // Output: { name: "Alice", age:
25, city: "New York" }
```

o In both examples, the spread operator is used to elements of an array or properties of an object, and you can add new items or properties.

In this chapter, you've learned about several key **ES6 (ECMAScript 2015)** features that make JavaScript more powerful and expressive. These features include:

- **let and const** for block-scoped variable declarations, which improve variable management and reduce errors.
- **Destructuring assignments** to extract values from arrays and objects concisely.

- **Template literals** for easier string interpolation and multi-line strings.

- **Default parameters** to assign fallback values to function parameters.

- **Rest and spread operators** for working with variable-length arguments and merging arrays or objects.

Mastering these ES6 features will make your JavaScript code cleaner, more efficient, and easier to maintain.

Chapter 14: Advanced Functions: Closures and Higher-Order Functions

---

In this chapter, we'll dive into some of the more advanced concepts in JavaScript functions, such as **closures** and **higher-order functions**. These concepts are crucial for understanding JavaScript's functional programming features and help you write more modular, efficient, and reusable code. We'll also explore how the **bind**, **call**, and **apply** methods work, along with **callback functions** and their use in real-world scenarios.

Understanding Closures and How They Work

A **closure** is a function that **remembers** its lexical environment (the variables in the scope where it was defined) even after it is executed outside of that environment. In simpler terms, a closure gives you access to an outer function's variables from an inner function.

Closures are a powerful feature in JavaScript, and they're often used to create private data or to preserve state.

1. **Creating a Closure**: When you define a function inside another function, the inner function has access to the

variables of the outer function. This is the foundation of closures.

Example:

javascript

```
function outerFunction() {
    let outerVariable = "I am from the outer function";

    function innerFunction() {
        console.log(outerVariable);   // Accessing outerVariable from the
outer scope
    }

    return innerFunction;
}

const closureExample = outerFunction();
closureExample();  // Output: I am from the outer function
```

- o In this example, innerFunction forms a closure because it has access to outerVariable, even though it is executed outside the scope of outerFunction.

2. **Why Closures Are Useful**: Closures are useful for creating functions with persistent state. They allow for data encapsulation, such as in **private variables** or **counters**.

Example (Counter with Closure):

javascript

```javascript
function createCounter() {
    let count = 0;
    return function() {
        count++;
        return count;
    };
}


const counter = createCounter();
console.log(counter());  // Output: 1
console.log(counter());  // Output: 2
console.log(counter());  // Output: 3
```

- o The inner function returned by createCounter() retains access to the count variable, even though createCounter() has finished executing. Each time counter() is called, it increments count, creating a persistent state.

Higher-Order Functions: Passing Functions as Arguments and Returning Functions

A **higher-order function** is a function that can either:

1. Take one or more functions as arguments.
2. Return a function as its result.

Higher-order functions are common in functional programming and allow for more abstract and reusable code.

1. **Passing Functions as Arguments**: Functions can be passed as arguments to other functions, enabling dynamic behavior.

    Example:

    javascript

    ```javascript
    function greet(name, callback) {
        console.log("Hello, " + name);
        callback();  // Calling the passed-in function
    }

    function sayGoodbye() {
        console.log("Goodbye!");
    }

    greet("Alice", sayGoodbye);  // Output: Hello, Alice  Goodbye!
    ```

    o   In this example, greet is a higher-order function that accepts another function (sayGoodbye) as a parameter and invokes it within its body.

2. **Returning Functions**: A function can return another function, which is often used in closures to create reusable behavior.

    Example:

javascript

```javascript
function multiplier(factor) {
  return function(number) {
    return number * factor;
  };
}

const double = multiplier(2);
console.log(double(5));  // Output: 10
const triple = multiplier(3);
console.log(triple(5));  // Output: 15
```

o In this example, the function multiplier returns a function that multiplies a given number by a specified factor. This allows for dynamic function creation based on the passed argument.

The Bind, Call, and Apply Methods

The bind, call, and apply methods allow you to control the this context of a function, making them useful for event handling, method borrowing, and function invocation with different this values.

1. **bind()**: The bind() method creates a new function that, when called, has its this value set to the provided object.

Example:

javascript

```javascript
function greet() {
    console.log("Hello, " + this.name);
}

const person = { name: "Alice" };
const greetPerson = greet.bind(person); // Creating a new function with
'this' bound to 'person'
greetPerson(); // Output: Hello, Alice
```

- o bind() does not immediately call the function; it returns a new function with the this context set to the specified value.

2. **call()**: The call() method invokes a function immediately, allowing you to specify the this context and pass arguments to the function.

Example:

javascript

```javascript
function greet(age) {
    console.log("Hello, " + this.name + ". You are " + age + " years old.");
}

const person = { name: "Bob" };
greet.call(person, 30); // Output: Hello, Bob. You are 30 years old.
```

o The call() method invokes greet() with this set to person, and the argument 30 is passed into the function.

3. **apply()**: The apply() method works like call(), but instead of passing arguments individually, you pass them as an array or array-like object.

Example:

javascript

```
function greet(age, city) {
    console.log("Hello, " + this.name + ". You are " + age + " years old
and live in " + city + ".");
}

const person = { name: "Charlie" };
greet.apply(person, [35, "New York"]);  // Output: Hello, Charlie. You
are 35 years old and live in New York.
```

o The apply() method allows you to pass the arguments as an array, making it convenient when dealing with an unknown number of arguments.

Callback Functions in Real-World Scenarios

Callbacks are widely used in real-world applications, especially in **asynchronous programming** (e.g., handling data fetching, user interactions, etc.). They are also essential in event handling, functional programming, and handling tasks that require a continuation.

1. **Example 1: Event Handling**: Event listeners in JavaScript use callback functions to execute when specific events (e.g., click, keypress) occur.

   Example:

   javascript

   ```
   document.getElementById("myButton").addEventListener("click",
   function() {
       alert("Button clicked!");
   });
   ```

2. **Example 2: Asynchronous Tasks (e.g., setTimeout)**: Callbacks are commonly used to handle asynchronous tasks, such as delays or fetching data.

   Example:

   javascript

   ```
   console.log("Start task");

   setTimeout(function() {
       console.log("Task completed after 3 seconds");
   }, 3000);
   ```

console.log("Task in progress...");

  o Here, the callback function passed to setTimeout runs after 3 seconds, allowing the asynchronous task to be handled without blocking the main thread.

3. **Example 3: Array Iteration with forEach**: The forEach() method is a higher-order function that takes a callback to execute for each element in an array.

Example:

javascript

```
const numbers = [1, 2, 3, 4];
numbers.forEach(function(num) {
    console.log(num * 2);  // Output: 2, 4, 6, 8
});
```

In this chapter, you've learned advanced concepts in JavaScript functions:

- **Closures**, which allow functions to retain access to their lexical scope even after execution.
- **Higher-order functions**, which enable passing functions as arguments and returning functions.

- The **bind**, **call**, and **apply** methods, which provide ways to control the this context and manage function invocation.

- **Callback functions**, which are integral for handling asynchronous tasks, events, and other dynamic behavior in JavaScript.

These concepts are central to JavaScript's functional programming features and will help you build more modular, reusable, and powerful applications.

Chapter 15: JavaScript Modules

JavaScript modules provide a powerful way to organize and manage code in large applications. By using modules, you can split your code into smaller, reusable pieces and import only the parts you need, improving maintainability, readability, and scalability. This chapter covers the fundamentals of **JavaScript modules**, including how to export and import functions and variables, the difference between **CommonJS** and **ES Modules**, and how to set up modular code for large projects.

Introduction to Modules in JavaScript

A **module** in JavaScript is a reusable piece of code that encapsulates functionality (such as functions, variables, or objects) and allows it to be shared across different parts of your application. Modules help avoid cluttering the global scope, preventing conflicts between different parts of the application.

Before ES6, JavaScript did not have a native module system, and developers relied on various workarounds like **IIFE** (Immediately Invoked Function Expressions) or external libraries like **RequireJS**. With the introduction of **ES6 modules**, JavaScript now has a built-in module system.

- **Modules** allow for the **export** of code from one file and **import** of it into another.
- ES6 modules are designed to be **static** (resolved at compile time), improving optimizations like tree shaking, where unused code is not included in the final build.

Exporting and Importing Functions and Variables

1. **Exporting Code**: In ES6, you can export functions, variables, and objects so they can be used in other files. There are two types of export: **named exports** and **default exports**.

   o **Named Exports**: Named exports allow you to export multiple functions, variables, or objects by their name.

   Example (Named Export):

   javascript

   ```
   // file: math.js
   export const add = (a, b) => a + b;
   export const subtract = (a, b) => a - b;
   ```
   In this example, both add and subtract are exported with their names. You can import them by matching the name exactly.

o **Default Export**: A default export allows you to export a single function, class, or object as the default export from a module. This can be imported without braces.

Example (Default Export):

javascript

```
// file: greet.js
const greet = (name) => {
    console.log(`Hello, ${name}!`);
};
```

export default greet;

The greet function is exported as the default export from greet.js.

2. **Importing Code**: To use the exported code in another file, you can use the import statement. You can import specific items or the default export.

o **Importing Named Exports**: To import named exports, you use the exact name of the exported item in curly braces.

Example (Named Import):

javascript

```
// file: app.js
import { add, subtract } from './math.js';

console.log(add(2, 3));       // Output: 5
console.log(subtract(5, 2));  // Output: 3
```

o **Importing Default Exports**: For default exports, you can give the imported value any name you like.

Example (Default Import):

javascript

```
// file: app.js
import greet from './greet.js';

greet("Alice"); // Output: Hello, Alice!
```

Since greet was exported as the default, you don't need to use curly braces when importing it.

3. **Importing All Exports**: If you want to import all exports from a module as a single object, you can use the * as syntax.

Example (Import All):

javascript

```
// file: app.js
import * as math from './math.js';
```

```
console.log(math.add(2, 3));     // Output: 5
console.log(math.subtract(5, 2)); // Output: 3
```

- o In this example, all the exports from math.js are grouped into a math object, allowing you to access them like math.add and math.subtract.

The Difference Between CommonJS and ES Modules

Before ES6, JavaScript used various module systems, with **CommonJS** being one of the most popular, especially in Node.js environments. The ES6 module system, however, is now the standard for both client-side and server-side JavaScript. Here's a comparison between the two:

1. **CommonJS**:
   - o CommonJS is synchronous, meaning it loads modules one at a time.
   - o Modules are exported using module.exports and imported with require().
   - o It is mostly used in Node.js environments.

Example (CommonJS):

javascript

// file: math.js

```
const add = (a, b) => a + b;
module.exports = { add };

// file: app.js
const math = require('./math.js');
console.log(math.add(2, 3)); // Output: 5
```

2. **ES Modules**:

- o ES6 modules are asynchronous, which allows for optimized bundling and loading of dependencies.
- o Modules are exported using export and imported with import.
- o ES6 modules are used natively in browsers and modern JavaScript environments.

Example (ES6 Modules):

javascript

```
// file: math.js
export const add = (a, b) => a + b;

// file: app.js
import { add } from './math.js';
console.log(add(2, 3));  // Output: 5
```

3. **Key Differences**:

- o **Syntax**: CommonJS uses module.exports and require(), whereas ES6 uses export and import.

- o **Synchronous vs. Asynchronous**: CommonJS modules are loaded synchronously, while ES6 modules are loaded asynchronously, which is more efficient for browser environments.

- o **Default Exports**: In CommonJS, module.exports can export a single object, while in ES6, you use export default for default exports.

Setting Up Modular Code for Large Projects

As projects grow larger, maintaining code without modularization can become difficult. Using modules helps in keeping code organized, reusable, and easier to manage. Here are some tips for setting up modular code in large JavaScript projects:

1. **Organize Code by Functionality**: Break your application into modules based on their functionality. For example:

   - o **auth.js**: Authentication logic
   - o **api.js**: API calls
   - o **utils.js**: Utility functions

2. **Use a Module Bundler**: In client-side JavaScript, you'll often use a module bundler like **Webpack** or **Parcel** to bundle your modules into a single file for efficient delivery to the browser.

- o With **Webpack**, you can configure how modules are bundled and optimize the build for production.
- o **Parcel** is a simpler bundler that automatically handles bundling and transformations.

3. **Use ES6 Modules for Better Optimization**: Since ES6 modules support **tree shaking**, bundlers can remove unused code from your final bundle, reducing file size.

4. **Create a Central Module for Imports**: For larger projects, you can create an index.js file that acts as a central point to import and export your application's modules. This reduces the need to import each module individually across different files.

Example (Central Module):

javascript

```
// file: index.js
export * from './auth.js';
export * from './api.js';
export * from './utils.js';
```

Then, you can import everything from index.js in other files:

javascript

```
// file: app.js
import { login, fetchData, formatDate } from './index.js';
```

5. **Consider Using Classes for Complex Modules**: For more complex logic, consider using classes to encapsulate functionality within a module.

Example:

javascript

```javascript
// file: user.js
class User {
  constructor(name, age) {
    this.name = name;
    this.age = age;
  }

  greet() {
    console.log(`Hello, ${this.name}!`);
  }
}

export default User;
```

- o In this example, User is a class that encapsulates user-related logic. The class can be easily imported and instantiated in other files.

In this chapter, you've learned about **JavaScript modules** and how they can help you organize and manage code in large applications. We covered how to **export** and **import** functions and variables, the differences between **CommonJS** and **ES Modules**, and how to structure modular code for large projects. By using modules, you can create cleaner, more maintainable code, which is essential as applications grow in size and complexity. Mastering modules is a key skill in modern JavaScript development.

Chapter 16: JavaScript and JSON (JavaScript Object Notation)

In modern web development, **JSON** (JavaScript Object Notation) is one of the most commonly used data formats for exchanging information between the client and the server. It is lightweight, easy to read and write, and can be easily parsed by both JavaScript and many other programming languages. This chapter will introduce you to **JSON**, how to **parse** and **stringify** JSON data, its role in **APIs**, and some practical use cases for JSON in web development.

Understanding JSON Format

JSON is a text-based format used to represent data as a series of key-value pairs. It is a language-independent data format, which means it can be used across different programming languages. Although JSON is inspired by JavaScript object syntax, it can be used by other languages like Python, Ruby, and Java.

JSON follows these basic rules:

1. **Data is represented in key-value pairs**: Each key is a string, followed by a colon (:), and then the associated value.

2. **Values can be strings, numbers, arrays, booleans, or other objects.**

3. **Objects are enclosed in curly braces** {}, and arrays are enclosed in square brackets [].

4. **Keys and string values must be enclosed in double quotes.**

Example JSON:

json

```json
{
  "name": "Alice",
  "age": 30,
  "isActive": true,
  "languages": ["English", "Spanish"],
  "address": {
    "street": "123 Main St",
    "city": "Somewhere"
  }
}
```

In this example:

- "name", "age", "isActive", and "languages" are keys.
- "Alice", 30, true, and the array ["English", "Spanish"] are values.
- The address is another object, which contains further key-value pairs.

Working with JSON: Parsing and Stringifying

JavaScript provides two built-in methods to work with JSON data: **JSON.parse()** and **JSON.stringify()**. These methods allow you to convert between JSON data and JavaScript objects.

1. **JSON.parse()**: Converts a JSON-formatted string into a JavaScript object.

   Example:

   javascript

   ```javascript
   const jsonString = '{"name": "Alice", "age": 30}';
   const jsonObject = JSON.parse(jsonString);

   console.log(jsonObject.name);  // Output: Alice
   console.log(jsonObject.age);  // Output: 30
   ```

   o   JSON.parse() takes a string in JSON format and converts it into a JavaScript object that you can manipulate like any other object.

2. **JSON.stringify()**: Converts a JavaScript object into a JSON-formatted string.

   Example:

   javascript

   ```javascript
   const person = {
   ```

```
    name: "Alice",
    age: 30
};
```

```
const jsonString = JSON.stringify(person);
console.log(jsonString);  // Output: {"name":"Alice","age":30}
```

- o JSON.stringify() is useful for sending data to a server or saving it in a JSON file, as it converts JavaScript objects into a format that can be transmitted over a network.

JSON in APIs and Web Development

JSON plays a critical role in **APIs** (Application Programming Interfaces) and web development. It is the most common format used for data exchange between clients (like web browsers) and servers.

1. **JSON in APIs**: When making requests to APIs, data is often sent and received in JSON format. For example, when you query a REST API, the response is typically a JSON object.

   Example: Fetching JSON data from an API using fetch():

   javascript

   fetch('https://jsonplaceholder.typicode.com/posts')

```
.then(response => response.json()) // Convert the response to JSON
.then(data => {
    console.log(data); // Output: Array of posts in JSON format
})
.catch(error => console.error('Error:', error));
```

- o In this example, the fetch() method is used to make a request to an API. The response is then parsed into a JavaScript object using response.json().

2. **Sending JSON Data to an API**: To send JSON data to an API (e.g., using a POST request), you can convert the JavaScript object into a JSON string using JSON.stringify().

Example: Sending JSON data to an API using fetch():

javascript

```
const newPost = {
    title: "New Post",
    body: "This is a new post.",
    userId: 1
};

fetch('https://jsonplaceholder.typicode.com/posts', {
    method: 'POST',
    headers: {
        'Content-Type': 'application/json'
    },
    body: JSON.stringify(newPost) // Convert JavaScript object to JSON
})
```

```
.then(response => response.json())
.then(data => console.log(data))   // Output: The newly created post object
.catch(error => console.error('Error:', error));
```

- o Here, we create a new post object, convert it to JSON format using JSON.stringify(), and send it to the API.

3. **Working with JSON and Asynchronous JavaScript**: Many times, APIs return JSON data asynchronously. JavaScript's **Promise** and **async/await** patterns are commonly used to handle asynchronous JSON data.

Example: Fetching JSON data with async/await:

javascript

```
async function fetchData() {
    try {
        const response = await fetch('https://jsonplaceholder.typicode.com/posts');
        const data = await response.json();
        console.log(data);  // Output: Array of posts in JSON format
    } catch (error) {
        console.error('Error:', error);
    }
}

fetchData();
```

o In this example, fetchData() fetches JSON data from an API asynchronously using the await keyword and processes it.

Practical Use Cases for JSON

JSON is used in a wide variety of scenarios in web development, ranging from server communication to data storage and configuration.

1. **Storing Configuration Data**: Many applications use JSON to store configuration data (such as API keys, theme settings, or user preferences) because it is easy to read and edit.

   Example:

   json

   ```
   {
       "theme": "dark",
       "language": "en",
       "notificationsEnabled": true
   }
   ```

2. **Storing and Transmitting User Data**: User data, such as profile information, preferences, or settings, is often stored in JSON format on the server or client-side (e.g., in local storage or cookies).

LEARNING JAVASCRIPT FOR BEGINNERS

Example: Storing user preferences in localStorage:

javascript

```
const userPreferences = {
  theme: "dark",
  fontSize: "16px"
};

localStorage.setItem("userPreferences",
JSON.stringify(userPreferences));
```

3. **Data Exchange in Web and Mobile Applications**: Web and mobile applications frequently exchange data between the client and server in JSON format, making it the ideal choice for communication. For example, social media platforms, e-commerce sites, and news apps rely on JSON to update content dynamically.

4. **Storing Large Data**: JSON is often used for storing and transmitting large amounts of structured data, such as datasets in databases or JSON-based document storage systems (e.g., **MongoDB**).

5. **Handling Nested Data Structures**: JSON allows for easy representation of hierarchical, nested data structures, which makes it useful for APIs that require complex data.

Example:

json

```json
{
  "id": 1,
  "name": "John Doe",
  "address": {
    "street": "123 Main St",
    "city": "Anytown",
    "zip": "12345"
  },
  "friends": [
    {"name": "Jane", "age": 28},
    {"name": "Mike", "age": 30}
  ]
}
```

In this chapter, you've learned about **JSON (JavaScript Object Notation)**, a lightweight and widely used format for data exchange. We covered the basics of working with JSON in JavaScript, including how to **parse** and **stringify** JSON data, how JSON is used in **APIs** for exchanging data between clients and servers, and practical use cases where JSON is employed. Understanding JSON is essential for modern web development, as it is the primary format for transmitting and storing data.

Chapter 17: Introduction to JavaScript Frameworks

JavaScript frameworks are essential tools for developers to build dynamic, interactive, and high-performance web applications. Frameworks provide structure and a set of pre-built tools, allowing developers to focus more on business logic and less on repetitive tasks. This chapter provides an overview of the most popular JavaScript frameworks—**React**, **Angular**, and **Vue.js**—and helps you choose the right framework for your project. We'll also explore the basic setup and concepts behind each framework and understand their importance in modern web development.

Overview of JavaScript Frameworks: React, Angular, Vue.js
There are many JavaScript frameworks, but **React**, **Angular**, and **Vue.js** are the most widely used today. Each has its unique features, and choosing the right one for your project depends on your needs and preferences.

1. **React**:
   o **React** is a **library** developed by Facebook, not technically a full-fledged framework. It focuses on

building user interfaces (UI) with reusable components.

o It is widely recognized for its **virtual DOM**, which optimizes rendering performance by updating only the changed parts of the UI.

o React is often used in combination with other libraries (e.g., React Router for routing, Redux for state management) to build full applications.

Key Features:

o Component-based architecture

o Virtual DOM for faster updates

o JSX syntax, which allows HTML and JavaScript to coexist in the same file

o One-way data binding

Example (Basic React Component):

jsx

```
import React from "react";

function App() {
   return <h1>Hello, React!</h1>;
}

export default App;
```

2. **Angular**:

- o **Angular** is a **full-fledged framework** developed by Google. It is a comprehensive solution for building single-page applications (SPAs).
- o Angular is known for its **two-way data binding**, **dependency injection**, and **modular architecture**. It uses TypeScript (a superset of JavaScript) for development.
- o Angular provides everything out of the box, including routing, form validation, HTTP client, and state management.

Key Features:

- o Two-way data binding for synchronized updates between UI and data
- o TypeScript support for better tooling and error checking
- o Built-in modules for routing, HTTP requests, and form handling
- o Directives for extending HTML behavior

Example (Basic Angular Component):

typescript

```typescript
import { Component } from '@angular/core';
```

```
@Component({
  selector: 'app-root',
  template: '<h1>Hello, Angular!</h1>',
  styleUrls: ['./app.component.css']
})
export class AppComponent { }
```

3. **Vue.js**:

   o **Vue.js** is a **progressive framework** created by Evan You. It is designed to be incrementally adoptable, meaning you can use Vue in small parts of a project or as a complete framework.

   o Vue is praised for its simplicity and flexibility. It combines the best features of both React and Angular—**reactive data binding** and **component-based architecture**—but with a gentle learning curve.

   o Vue provides a great developer experience with its clear documentation and flexible ecosystem.

Key Features:

   o Reactive data binding
   o Component-based architecture
   o Lightweight and flexible

o   Built-in tools for routing and state management (Vue Router and Vuex)

Example (Basic Vue.js Component):

html

```
<template>
  <h1>Hello, Vue.js!</h1>
</template>

<script>
export default {
  name: 'App',
};
</script>
```

Choosing the Right Framework for Your Project

Selecting the right framework depends on various factors such as the size and complexity of the project, the team's experience, and the desired features. Below are some guidelines to help you choose between React, Angular, and Vue.js:

1. **When to Choose React**:
   o   **Complex and dynamic UIs**: React is ideal for projects that require fast, dynamic, and interactive user interfaces, especially where performance is critical.

- o **Component-based architecture**: React's component model fits well for large applications with many reusable parts.
- o **Flexibility**: React allows you to choose your tools for routing, state management, etc., making it a flexible choice for developers who want to tailor their stack.

2. **When to Choose Angular**:
   - o **Full-scale enterprise applications**: Angular is a good choice for large applications that require a comprehensive solution with built-in tools for routing, forms, HTTP requests, and more.
   - o **TypeScript support**: If your team prefers or requires TypeScript for better tooling and type-checking, Angular's use of TypeScript is a big advantage.
   - o **Two-way data binding**: Angular's two-way data binding is useful when you need synchronized updates between the model and the view.

3. **When to Choose Vue.js**:
   - o **Simplicity and flexibility**: Vue.js is the best choice if you are looking for something that's easy to learn, with a gentle learning curve.
   - o **Small to medium projects**: Vue works great for small to medium-scale applications, and its flexibility allows you to incrementally adopt it.

o **Integration with existing projects**: If you're adding interactivity to a legacy app, Vue is easy to integrate with existing projects due to its progressive nature.

Basic Setup and Understanding of Each Framework

1. **React Setup**: React can be set up using the **Create React App** tool, which provides a fully configured environment for React projects.

Setting up React:

o Install Node.js if you haven't already.

o Use npx to create a React app:

bash

```
npx create-react-app my-app
cd my-app
npm start
```

Understanding React Basics:

o React components are written as functions or classes. The function components are simpler and recommended for new projects.

o   JSX is used to define the component's UI in a syntax that resembles HTML, but you can embed JavaScript expressions inside curly braces {}.

2. **Angular Setup**: Angular projects are created using the **Angular CLI**, which helps set up the project and manage development tasks.

Setting up Angular:

o   Install Node.js if you haven't already.

o   Install Angular CLI globally:

bash

```
npm install -g @angular/cli
```

o   Create a new Angular project:

bash

```
ng new my-app
cd my-app
ng serve
```

Understanding Angular Basics:

o   Angular uses **components**, **services**, and **modules** as its core building blocks.

- o Angular applications are built around **modules** that organize different parts of the app, and **components** define the views.
- o Angular applications use **two-way data binding** to automatically synchronize the data between the model and the view.

3. **Vue.js Setup**: Vue.js is easy to set up and can be integrated into any project. The **Vue CLI** helps manage projects and dependencies.

Setting up Vue.js:

- o Install Node.js if you haven't already.
- o Install Vue CLI globally:

bash

npm install -g @vue/cli

- o Create a new Vue project:

bash

vue create my-app
cd my-app
npm run serve

Understanding Vue Basics:

o Vue uses **components**, similar to React, to build the UI.

o Vue's **reactivity system** automatically updates the DOM when the data changes, making it easy to bind data to the UI.

o Vue uses a **template-based syntax**, and you define the structure, logic, and style in one file.

The Importance of Frameworks in Modern Web Development

In modern web development, frameworks provide several key benefits:

1. **Efficiency and Productivity**: Frameworks come with pre-configured tools, utilities, and libraries that save time and reduce the amount of boilerplate code required. This allows developers to focus on the unique aspects of their application instead of reinventing the wheel.

2. **Maintainability**: Frameworks encourage the use of best practices like component-based architecture and modularity, making it easier to maintain and scale applications over time.

3. **Performance**: Modern frameworks like React, Angular, and Vue come with built-in optimizations, such as virtual DOM (React), two-way data binding (Angular), and reactivity systems (Vue). These features ensure that updates to the user

interface happen efficiently without unnecessary re-rendering.

4. **Community and Ecosystem**: Each framework has a large community of developers contributing to its ecosystem, providing tutorials, libraries, and tools that can help speed up development. The rich ecosystems of frameworks offer solutions to common problems, such as routing, state management, and form handling.

5. **Cross-Platform Development**: Some JavaScript frameworks, like **React Native** (based on React) and **Ionic** (based on Angular), allow for building cross-platform mobile applications, enabling you to use the same framework for web and mobile development.

In this chapter, we explored the three most popular JavaScript frameworks: **React**, **Angular**, and **Vue.js**. Each has its strengths, and the choice between them depends on factors like project size, complexity, and developer preference. Frameworks are essential in modern web development, as they help streamline development, improve performance, and make code more maintainable. By understanding the basics of each framework, you can choose the right one for your next project and be well-equipped to build scalable, dynamic applications.

Chapter 18: JavaScript and Local Storage

In modern web development, managing state and storing data locally on the client-side is essential for providing a smooth user experience. **Local Storage** and **Session Storage** are two web storage mechanisms that allow you to store data in the browser. This chapter will introduce you to **localStorage** and **sessionStorage**, explore how to store and retrieve data, discuss use cases for persistent data storage, and explain how to work with **JSON** data in localStorage.

Introduction to localStorage and sessionStorage

Both **localStorage** and **sessionStorage** are part of the **Web Storage API** and allow developers to store data in the browser's local storage. They are similar in that they both allow storing data as key-value pairs, but they differ in terms of scope and persistence.

1. **localStorage**:
    - **Persistence**: Data stored in **localStorage** is persistent and does not expire. It remains in the browser until explicitly deleted by the user or through JavaScript.

- o **Scope**: Data stored in **localStorage** is accessible across different tabs and windows of the same origin.
- o **Capacity**: The data limit for **localStorage** is generally larger than that of cookies (around 5-10MB, depending on the browser).

2. **sessionStorage**:

- o **Persistence**: Data stored in **sessionStorage** is only available for the duration of the page session. It is cleared when the page is closed or the session ends.
- o **Scope**: **sessionStorage** data is specific to the tab or window, meaning data is not shared across different tabs or windows of the same origin.
- o **Capacity**: The data limit for **sessionStorage** is similar to **localStorage**, but the data is only available within the session.

Storing and Retrieving Data from the Browser

1. **Storing Data in localStorage**: You can use the localStorage.setItem() method to store data in localStorage. This method requires two arguments: a key (string) and a value (string).

Example:

javascript

```
// Storing data in localStorage
localStorage.setItem('username', 'JohnDoe');
```

- In this example, the key is 'username' and the value is 'JohnDoe'.

2. **Retrieving Data from localStorage**: You can use the localStorage.getItem() method to retrieve data by its key.

   Example:

   javascript

   ```
   // Retrieving data from localStorage
   const username = localStorage.getItem('username');
   console.log(username);  // Output: JohnDoe
   ```

   - If the key doesn't exist in **localStorage**, getItem() returns null.

3. **Removing Data from localStorage**: Use the localStorage.removeItem() method to remove data associated with a particular key.

   Example:

   javascript

   ```
   // Removing data from localStorage
   localStorage.removeItem('username');
   ```

4. **Clearing All Data from localStorage**: To remove all key-value pairs stored in **localStorage**, use the localStorage.clear() method.

Example:

javascript

// Clearing all data from localStorage
localStorage.clear();

- This method will clear all stored data, so use it carefully.

Use Cases for Persistent Data Storage

localStorage and **sessionStorage** can be used in various scenarios where storing and retrieving client-side data is necessary. Here are some practical use cases for persistent data storage:

1. **User Preferences**: Store user preferences (such as language settings, theme, or display options) in **localStorage** to persist the settings across sessions. This enhances the user experience by remembering settings even after the browser is closed.

Example:

javascript

```
localStorage.setItem('theme', 'dark');
```

2. **Form Data**: If the user is filling out a form, you can store the form data in **localStorage** to preserve it in case the page is accidentally refreshed or closed. This way, users don't lose their progress.

   Example:

   javascript

   ```
   // Store form data
   const formData = {
       name: 'Alice',
       email: 'alice@example.com'
   };
   localStorage.setItem('formData', JSON.stringify(formData));
   ```

3. **Authentication Tokens**: After a user logs in, you can store an authentication token or session ID in **localStorage** to maintain the user's session across page reloads or tab sessions.

   Example:

   javascript

   ```
   localStorage.setItem('authToken', '12345abcde');
   ```

4. **Shopping Cart**: For e-commerce websites, you can store items in the shopping cart in **localStorage** to ensure that the user's cart persists even if they leave and return later.

Example:

javascript

```
const cartItems = [
    { id: 1, name: 'Laptop', price: 1000 },
    { id: 2, name: 'Phone', price: 500 }
];
localStorage.setItem('cart', JSON.stringify(cartItems));
```

5. **Offline Storage**: **localStorage** can be used to store data for offline use in progressive web apps (PWAs). When the user is offline, you can load the app data from **localStorage**.

Working with JSON Data in localStorage

Often, the data you need to store in **localStorage** is more complex than simple strings, such as objects or arrays. Since **localStorage** only accepts strings as values, you must use **JSON.stringify()** to convert JavaScript objects to JSON strings before storing them, and use **JSON.parse()** to convert JSON strings back into JavaScript objects when retrieving them.

1. **Storing JSON Data**: Use JSON.stringify() to convert an object or array to a string before storing it in **localStorage**.

   Example:

   javascript

   ```javascript
   const user = {
     name: 'Alice',
     age: 30
   };
   localStorage.setItem('user', JSON.stringify(user));
   ```

2. **Retrieving and Parsing JSON Data**: When retrieving the data, use JSON.parse() to convert the string back into a JavaScript object.

   Example:

   javascript

   ```javascript
   const storedUser = JSON.parse(localStorage.getItem('user'));
   console.log(storedUser);  // Output: { name: 'Alice', age: 30 }
   ```

   o   If the data doesn't exist or can't be parsed, JSON.parse() will throw an error. It's good practice to handle this with a try...catch block.

   Example with Error Handling:

javascript

```javascript
try {
  const storedUser = JSON.parse(localStorage.getItem('user'));
  console.log(storedUser);
} catch (error) {
  console.error('Error parsing JSON from localStorage:', error);
}
```

Best Practices for Using localStorage

1. **Limit the amount of data stored**: While **localStorage** allows you to store large amounts of data (typically up to 5-10MB depending on the browser), storing too much data can slow down the browser or cause performance issues. Always keep track of how much data you're storing.

2. **Use for non-sensitive data**: Since **localStorage** is accessible through JavaScript and is not encrypted, it's not a good place to store sensitive information like passwords or authentication tokens. Use more secure storage options (e.g., cookies with HttpOnly flags) for sensitive data.

3. **Handle JSON parsing errors gracefully**: When dealing with JSON, ensure that you handle parsing errors to avoid breaking your app. Using a try...catch block around JSON.parse() is a good practice.

4. **Remember to clean up**: Remove unnecessary data from **localStorage** when it is no longer needed. Over time, unused data can accumulate and affect performance.

In this chapter, you've learned how to work with **localStorage** and **sessionStorage**, two essential features of the Web Storage API that allow you to store and retrieve data in the browser. We explored practical use cases for **persistent data storage**, such as storing user preferences, form data, authentication tokens, and shopping cart items. Additionally, you've learned how to handle **JSON data** in **localStorage** and ensure that objects and arrays are correctly serialized and deserialized. By mastering **localStorage**, you can improve the user experience in your web applications by persisting important data across sessions and page reloads.

Chapter 19: JavaScript in the Real World: Practical Projects

JavaScript is a powerful tool for building dynamic, interactive web applications. In this chapter, we'll explore how to apply JavaScript to build practical, real-world projects. We'll focus on creating a **to-do list application**, work with forms and validate user input, use JavaScript to fetch and display data from APIs, and integrate JavaScript with HTML and CSS to create engaging and functional web pages.

Building a To-Do List Application

A **to-do list application** is a classic project for practicing JavaScript skills. It involves managing tasks, adding new tasks, deleting tasks, and marking tasks as complete. This project allows you to work with **DOM manipulation**, **event handling**, and **localStorage**.

1. **Basic Structure**:
    - **HTML**: A simple structure for displaying the to-do list and buttons for adding and removing tasks.
    - **CSS**: Styling to make the app user-friendly and visually appealing.

- o **JavaScript**: Logic to add, delete, and mark tasks as complete, as well as saving tasks in **localStorage** to persist data.

2. **HTML (Basic Structure)**:

html

```html
<div id="app">
  <h1>To-Do List</h1>
  <input type="text" id="taskInput" placeholder="Add a new task" />
  <button id="addTaskBtn">Add Task</button>
  <ul id="taskList"></ul>
</div>
```

3. **CSS (Basic Styling)**:

css

```css
#app {
  width: 300px;
  margin: 0 auto;
  padding: 20px;
  background-color: #f4f4f4;
  border-radius: 8px;
}

ul {
  list-style-type: none;
  padding: 0;
}
```

```css
li {
    padding: 10px;
    background-color: #fff;
    margin: 5px 0;
    border-radius: 5px;
}

.completed {
    text-decoration: line-through;
}
```

4. JavaScript (Task Logic):

javascript

```javascript
const taskInput = document.getElementById('taskInput');
const addTaskBtn = document.getElementById('addTaskBtn');
const taskList = document.getElementById('taskList');

// Load tasks from localStorage
const loadTasks = () => {
    const tasks = JSON.parse(localStorage.getItem('tasks')) || [];
    taskList.innerHTML = '';
    tasks.forEach((task, index) => {
        const li = document.createElement('li');
        li.textContent = task.text;
        if (task.completed) li.classList.add('completed');
        li.addEventListener('click', () => toggleTask(index));
        const deleteBtn = document.createElement('button');
```

```
      deleteBtn.textContent = 'Delete';
      deleteBtn.addEventListener('click', (e) => {
        e.stopPropagation();
        deleteTask(index);
      });
      li.appendChild(deleteBtn);
      taskList.appendChild(li);
    });
};


// Add a new task
const addTask = () => {
    const taskText = taskInput.value.trim();
    if (taskText) {
      const tasks = JSON.parse(localStorage.getItem('tasks')) || [];
      tasks.push({ text: taskText, completed: false });
      localStorage.setItem('tasks', JSON.stringify(tasks));
      taskInput.value = '';
      loadTasks();
    }
};


// Toggle task completion
const toggleTask = (index) => {
    const tasks = JSON.parse(localStorage.getItem('tasks')) || [];
    tasks[index].completed = !tasks[index].completed;
    localStorage.setItem('tasks', JSON.stringify(tasks));
    loadTasks();
};
```

```
// Delete a task
const deleteTask = (index) => {
    const tasks = JSON.parse(localStorage.getItem('tasks')) || [];
    tasks.splice(index, 1);
    localStorage.setItem('tasks', JSON.stringify(tasks));
    loadTasks();
};


addTaskBtn.addEventListener('click', addTask);


loadTasks();  // Initial load of tasks
```

- o **Features**:
  - Tasks can be added by typing in the input field and clicking "Add Task".
  - Tasks can be marked as completed by clicking on them.
  - Tasks can be deleted by clicking the "Delete" button.
  - Tasks are saved in **localStorage** and persist after page reloads.

Working with Forms and Validating User Input

Forms are integral to most web applications, whether they involve user authentication, contact forms, or data submission. Validating user input is essential to ensure that the data submitted is correct, complete, and safe.

1. **Creating a Basic Form**: Let's build a simple form for submitting a user's name and email.

   HTML:

   html

```html
<form id="userForm">
    <label for="name">Name:</label>
    <input type="text" id="name" required />
    <label for="email">Email:</label>
    <input type="email" id="email" required />
    <button type="submit">Submit</button>
</form>
<div id="error-message"></div>
```

2. **JavaScript for Form Validation**:
   - Validate that the input fields are not empty.
   - Ensure the email is in the correct format.

   Example:

   javascript

```javascript
const form = document.getElementById('userForm');
const nameInput = document.getElementById('name');
const emailInput = document.getElementById('email');
```

```
const errorMessage = document.getElementById('error-message');

form.addEventListener('submit', (event) => {
  event.preventDefault();
  errorMessage.textContent = ''; // Clear previous error messages

  // Check if name is empty
  if (!nameInput.value.trim()) {
    errorMessage.textContent = 'Name is required!';
    return;
  }

  // Check if email is valid
  const emailRegex = /^[a-zA-Z0-9._-]+@[a-zA-Z0-9.-]+\.[a-zA-Z]{2,4}$/;
  if (!emailRegex.test(emailInput.value)) {
    errorMessage.textContent = 'Please enter a valid email!';
    return;
  }

  alert('Form submitted successfully!');
  nameInput.value = '';
  emailInput.value = '';
});
```

- o **Explanation**: This form will display error messages if the name field is empty or if the email is not in the correct format.

Using JavaScript to Fetch and Display Data from APIs

Fetching data from APIs is a common use case for JavaScript. Many modern web applications rely on APIs to fetch data dynamically, such as retrieving user information, displaying news articles, or loading images.

1. **Fetching Data with the fetch() API**:
   - o The fetch() method is used to make HTTP requests and retrieve data from an API.
   - o It returns a **Promise** that resolves to the response of the request.

Example:

javascript

```
const url = 'https://jsonplaceholder.typicode.com/posts';

fetch(url)
    .then(response => response.json())
    .then(data => {
      console.log(data);  // Display the fetched data
      const postList = document.getElementById('post-list');
      data.forEach(post => {
        const listItem = document.createElement('li');
        listItem.textContent = post.title;
        postList.appendChild(listItem);
      });
    })
```

```
.catch(error => console.error('Error fetching data:', error));
```

- o **Explanation**: This example fetches a list of posts from a public API and displays the titles in an unordered list (<ul>).

Integrating JavaScript with HTML and CSS

JavaScript is often used to manipulate the DOM (Document Object Model) to update the content of a webpage. It can also interact with CSS to change styles dynamically.

1. **Changing Styles Dynamically**: You can change the style of elements dynamically with JavaScript by modifying the style property.

   Example:

   javascript

   ```
   const button = document.getElementById('changeColorButton');

   button.addEventListener('click', () => {
       document.body.style.backgroundColor = 'lightblue';
   });
   ```

   - o **Explanation**: When the user clicks the button, the background color of the page changes to light blue.

2. **Toggling CSS Classes**: You can toggle CSS classes on elements to change their styles without directly modifying the inline style.

Example:

javascript

```
const toggleButton = document.getElementById('toggleButton');
const box = document.getElementById('box');

toggleButton.addEventListener('click', () => {
  box.classList.toggle('active');
});
```

CSS:

css

```
.active {
  background-color: yellow;
  width: 200px;
  height: 200px;
}
```

- o **Explanation**: This example uses a button to toggle the active class on a div, changing its size and color when clicked.

In this chapter, you've learned how to apply JavaScript to real-world projects, starting with a **to-do list application** that demonstrates DOM manipulation, **form handling**, **user input validation**, and **localStorage**. We also explored how to use JavaScript to **fetch data from APIs**, display it on the page, and interact with HTML and CSS to create dynamic and responsive applications. By building these practical projects, you've gained valuable experience in integrating JavaScript with other web technologies, setting you up for building more complex and interactive web applications.

Chapter 20: Working with Dates and Time in JavaScript

Handling dates and times is an essential part of web development. Whether you are building a calendar, scheduling system, or tracking events, JavaScript provides several methods to manage dates and times. In this chapter, we'll explore how to create and manipulate **Date** objects, format dates and times, perform date calculations, and work with **timezones**. Additionally, we'll look at third-party libraries that simplify date and time handling.

Creating and Manipulating Date Objects

JavaScript provides the built-in Date object to represent dates and times. The Date object can be created in various ways to represent the current date and time, or a specific point in the past or future.

1. **Creating a Date Object**:
   - o To create a Date object representing the current date and time, use the new Date() constructor.

   Example:

   javascript

```javascript
const currentDate = new Date();
console.log(currentDate);  // Output: Current date and time (e.g., Wed Sep 29 2021 14:43:52 GMT-0400 (Eastern Daylight Time))
```

2. **Creating a Date Object with a Specific Date and Time**: You can pass specific date and time parameters to the Date constructor. The format is new Date(year, monthIndex, day, hours, minutes, seconds, milliseconds).

Example:

javascript

```javascript
const specificDate = new Date(2022, 4, 15, 10, 30, 0);  // May 15, 2022, at 10:30 AM
console.log(specificDate);  // Output: Sun May 15 2022 10:30:00 GMT-0400 (Eastern Daylight Time)
```

   o **Note**: In JavaScript, months are zero-indexed (January is 0, February is 1, and so on), so May is represented by 4.

3. **Getting the Current Date Components**: You can extract specific components of a Date object, such as the year, month, day, etc., using various get methods.

Example:

javascript

```
const today = new Date();
console.log(today.getFullYear()); // Get the current year
console.log(today.getMonth());    // Get the current month (zero-indexed)
console.log(today.getDate());     // Get the current day of the month
console.log(today.getHours());    // Get the current hour
console.log(today.getMinutes());  // Get the current minutes
console.log(today.getSeconds());  // Get the current seconds
```

4. **Setting Date Components**: You can also modify specific parts of a Date object using the set methods.

   Example:

   javascript

```
const date = new Date();
date.setFullYear(2023);  // Set the year to 2023
date.setMonth(5);        // Set the month to June (index 5)
date.setDate(20);        // Set the day of the month to 20
console.log(date);       // Output: A new date with the updated values
```

Formatting Dates and Time

JavaScript's Date object has limited built-in functionality for formatting dates. However, you can easily extract components of the date and manually format them or use third-party libraries for more complex formatting.

1. **Manually Formatting Dates**: You can format dates by combining the various get methods into a custom format.

   Example (Custom Format):

   javascript

   ```
   const date = new Date();
   const formattedDate = `${date.getDate()}/${date.getMonth() + 1}/${date.getFullYear()}`;
   console.log(formattedDate);  // Output: 29/9/2021 (for example)
   ```

2. **Using toLocaleDateString()**: The toLocaleDateString() method allows you to format the date based on the locale and options.

   Example:

   javascript

   ```
   const date = new Date();
   const formattedDate = date.toLocaleDateString('en-US');    // MM/DD/YYYY format
   console.log(formattedDate);  // Output: 09/29/2021
   ```

   o   You can also pass additional options for more control over the format.

   javascript

   ```
   const formattedDate = date.toLocaleDateString('en-GB', {
   ```

```
weekday: 'long',
year: 'numeric',
month: 'long',
day: 'numeric'
});
console.log(formattedDate);  // Output: Wednesday, 29 September 2021
```

Performing Date Calculations

JavaScript makes it easy to perform date calculations such as adding or subtracting days, months, or years.

1. **Adding or Subtracting Time**: You can manipulate a Date object by modifying its time (milliseconds). For example, to add days or subtract months, you can use the setDate(), setMonth(), and setFullYear() methods.

   Example (Adding Days):

   javascript

   ```
   const today = new Date();
   const futureDate = new Date(today);
   futureDate.setDate(today.getDate() + 10);  // Add 10 days
   console.log(futureDate);  // Output: Date 10 days from today
   ```

   Example (Subtracting Months):

   javascript

   ```
   const today = new Date();
   ```

```javascript
const pastDate = new Date(today);
pastDate.setMonth(today.getMonth() - 3);  // Subtract 3 months
console.log(pastDate);  // Output: Date 3 months ago
```

2. **Comparing Dates**: JavaScript's Date objects can be compared by converting them into milliseconds. You can use relational operators like <, >, and === to compare dates.

Example:

javascript

```javascript
const date1 = new Date('2021-09-01');
const date2 = new Date('2021-09-15');
console.log(date1 < date2);  // Output: true
```

3. **Calculating the Difference Between Dates**: You can calculate the difference between two dates by subtracting one Date object from another. This will give you the difference in **milliseconds**.

Example:

javascript

```javascript
const startDate = new Date('2021-09-01');
const endDate = new Date('2021-09-10');
const timeDiff = endDate - startDate;
const daysDiff = timeDiff / (1000 * 3600 * 24);  // Convert milliseconds to days
```

console.log(daysDiff); // Output: 9

Timezone Handling and Working with Third-Party Libraries

Timezone handling in JavaScript can be tricky, especially when dealing with global applications. JavaScript's Date object uses the browser's local timezone by default, which might lead to inconsistencies when working with time zones or when converting between different time zones.

1. **Using toLocaleString() for Timezone Formatting**: The toLocaleString() method allows you to format a date according to a specific time zone.

    Example:

    javascript

    ```javascript
    const date = new Date();
    const timeInNewYork = date.toLocaleString('en-US', {
        timeZone: 'America/New_York'
    });
    console.log(timeInNewYork); // Output: New York local time
    ```

2. **Working with Third-Party Libraries**: For more advanced timezone handling and date formatting, many developers use third-party libraries like **Moment.js** (now in maintenance mode), **date-fns**, or **Luxon**.

o **Moment.js**: A popular library that makes it easier to parse, validate, manipulate, and display dates in JavaScript.

Example (Using Moment.js):

javascript

```
const moment = require('moment');
const formattedDate = moment().format('MMMM Do YYYY, h:mm:ss a');
console.log(formattedDate);  // Output: September 29th 2021, 2:43:52 pm
```

o **Luxon**: A library that works well with time zones and provides a modern API to handle dates and times.

Example (Using Luxon):

javascript

```
const { DateTime } = require('luxon');
const dt = DateTime.now().setZone('America/New_York');
console.log(dt.toString());       // Output: 2021-09-29T14:43:52.123-04:00
```

o **date-fns**: A lightweight and modular library for date manipulation.

Example (Using date-fns):

javascript

```javascript
const { format } = require('date-fns');
const formattedDate = format(new Date(), 'MMMM dd, yyyy');
console.log(formattedDate);  // Output: September 29, 2021
```

In this chapter, you've learned how to work with **dates and times** in JavaScript. We covered the basics of creating and manipulating Date objects, formatting dates and times for different locales, performing date calculations, and handling timezones. Additionally, we explored third-party libraries like **Moment.js**, **Luxon**, and **date-fns**, which provide enhanced functionality for handling dates and times in JavaScript. Understanding these concepts is essential for building applications that deal with time-sensitive data, such as event scheduling, time zone conversions, or logging.

Chapter 21: JavaScript and Web Storage

The **Web Storage API** provides a way to store data locally within the user's browser. This is a powerful tool for modern web applications, as it allows for persistent data storage that is easily accessible by JavaScript, without the need to rely on server-side storage. This chapter will introduce you to the **Web Storage API**, explain how to store and retrieve data using **localStorage** and **sessionStorage**, and highlight the differences between **cookies** and web storage. Finally, we will explore common **use cases** for web storage in real-world web applications.

Introduction to Web Storage API

The **Web Storage API** is a simple way for web applications to store data in the browser. It allows you to store data as **key-value pairs**, and the data can persist across page reloads, or even across different sessions, depending on the storage mechanism used. The Web Storage API consists of two primary components:

1. **localStorage**:
   o Stores data with no expiration time.
   o Data is persistent across browser sessions and remains until explicitly deleted.

2. **sessionStorage**:

  - o Stores data for the duration of the page session.
  - o Data is cleared when the page or tab is closed.

Both mechanisms are part of the **window.localStorage** and **window.sessionStorage** objects, respectively.

Key Advantages of Web Storage:

- Data is stored locally, improving performance by reducing server load.
- Easier to use than cookies, and doesn't involve sending data with every HTTP request.
- Larger storage capacity compared to cookies.

Storing and Retrieving Data Using localStorage and sessionStorage

1. **Storing Data**: You can store data in both **localStorage** and **sessionStorage** using the setItem() method, which takes a key and a value.

  - o **Storing Data in localStorage**:

    javascript

    localStorage.setItem('username', 'JohnDoe');

```javascript
localStorage.setItem('isLoggedIn', true);
```

o **Storing Data in sessionStorage**:

javascript

```javascript
sessionStorage.setItem('sessionToken', 'abc123');
sessionStorage.setItem('isUserActive', true);
```

o **Note**: Data in both localStorage and sessionStorage must be stored as strings. To store objects or arrays, you need to convert them to JSON strings using JSON.stringify().

javascript

```javascript
const user = { name: "Alice", age: 25 };
localStorage.setItem('user', JSON.stringify(user));
```

2. **Retrieving Data**: You can retrieve data from **localStorage** and **sessionStorage** using the getItem() method, which returns the value stored under a specific key.

o **Retrieving Data from localStorage**:

javascript

```javascript
const username = localStorage.getItem('username');
const isLoggedIn = localStorage.getItem('isLoggedIn');
console.log(username, isLoggedIn); // Output: JohnDoe true
```

o **Retrieving Data from sessionStorage**:

javascript

```javascript
const sessionToken = sessionStorage.getItem('sessionToken');
const isUserActive = sessionStorage.getItem('isUserActive');
console.log(sessionToken, isUserActive);   // Output: abc123 true
```

o **Retrieving JSON Data**: If you stored an object as a JSON string, you can convert it back into an object using JSON.parse().

javascript

```javascript
const storedUser = JSON.parse(localStorage.getItem('user'));
console.log(storedUser.name); // Output: Alice
```

3. **Removing Data**: To remove data, you can use the removeItem() method.

o **Remove Data from localStorage**:

javascript

```javascript
localStorage.removeItem('username');
```

o **Remove Data from sessionStorage**:

javascript

LEARNING JAVASCRIPT FOR BEGINNERS

sessionStorage.removeItem('sessionToken');

4. **Clearing All Data**: You can clear all data from **localStorage** or **sessionStorage** using the clear() method.

    o   **Clear all localStorage data**:

        javascript

        localStorage.clear();

    o   **Clear all sessionStorage data**:

        javascript

        sessionStorage.clear();

Differences Between Cookies and Web Storage

Cookies and web storage are both used for storing data on the client-side, but they differ significantly in terms of features, usage, and limitations.

1. **Storage Capacity**:
    o   **Cookies**: Typically can store up to 4KB of data per domain.
    o   **Web Storage**: **localStorage** and **sessionStorage** can store much larger amounts of data, typically around 5-10MB per domain, depending on the browser.

2. **Data Transmission**:

   o **Cookies**: Cookies are sent with every HTTP request to the server, including requests for images, stylesheets, and other resources. This can slow down performance if cookies contain large amounts of data.

   o **Web Storage**: Data stored in **localStorage** and **sessionStorage** is never sent to the server with HTTP requests, improving performance.

3. **Expiration**:

   o **Cookies**: Cookies have an expiration date that can be set by the developer. If no expiration is specified, the cookie is deleted when the session ends.

   o **Web Storage**: Data in **localStorage** does not have an expiration time and remains until deleted by the developer. Data in **sessionStorage** is automatically cleared when the page or tab is closed.

4. **Accessibility**:

   o **Cookies**: Cookies are sent to the server automatically, but they can also be accessed via JavaScript (unless the cookie is set with the HttpOnly flag).

   o **Web Storage**: Data stored in **localStorage** and **sessionStorage** can only be accessed via JavaScript running in the same origin (domain).

5. **Security**:

- o **Cookies**: Cookies can be secured with the Secure flag (only sent over HTTPS) and the HttpOnly flag (not accessible by JavaScript).

- o **Web Storage**: **localStorage** and **sessionStorage** do not have these security flags. Data stored in **Web Storage** can be accessed by any script running on the same domain, so it's not suitable for storing sensitive information such as passwords.

Use Cases in Web Applications

Web storage is particularly useful in scenarios where you need to store data on the client side for improving the user experience, enabling offline functionality, or reducing the number of requests to the server.

1. **Persisting User Preferences**: Store user preferences, such as language settings, theme selection, or layout preferences, in **localStorage** to remember the settings across sessions.

   Example:

   javascript

   ```javascript
   const theme = 'dark';
   localStorage.setItem('theme', theme);
   ```

2. **Shopping Cart**: For e-commerce websites, store the shopping cart items in **localStorage** to persist the cart across page reloads or sessions. This way, users don't lose their items when they return to the site.

Example:

javascript

```
const cart = [
    { id: 1, name: 'Laptop', price: 1000 },
    { id: 2, name: 'Phone', price: 500 }
];
localStorage.setItem('cart', JSON.stringify(cart));
```

3. **Offline Storage**: **localStorage** can be used in **Progressive Web Apps (PWAs)** to store data for offline use. You can save information when the user is online and retrieve it later when they are offline.

4. **Authentication Tokens**: Store session tokens or authentication keys in **sessionStorage** to maintain the user's session during navigation within the same tab. However, avoid storing sensitive information in **localStorage** for security reasons.

Example:

javascript

```
sessionStorage.setItem('authToken', 'abcd1234');
```

5. **Form Data Persistence**: Use **localStorage** or **sessionStorage** to store form data temporarily, so users don't lose their progress if they accidentally refresh or navigate away from the page.

6. **Analytics**: Use **localStorage** to store user interactions or preferences for analytics purposes. For instance, you could track user visits to specific pages or features, and this data could be used to enhance the user experience.

In this chapter, you've learned about the **Web Storage API**, which provides powerful tools for storing data on the client side with **localStorage** and **sessionStorage**. These storage mechanisms offer larger capacity and better performance compared to cookies, and they're ideal for use cases like persisting user preferences, shopping carts, and authentication tokens. Understanding the differences between cookies and web storage is essential for choosing the right storage solution for your application. By leveraging the Web Storage API, you can improve user experience, reduce server load, and enable offline functionality in your web applications.

Chapter 22: Security and Best Practices in JavaScript

Security is a critical aspect of web development. JavaScript, being one of the most widely used programming languages for building interactive websites and applications, is often a target for various attacks. Understanding common security vulnerabilities in JavaScript and learning how to protect your applications is essential to creating safe and reliable web applications. In this chapter, we will explore common security vulnerabilities, how to prevent **XSS (Cross-Site Scripting)** attacks, the importance of sanitizing user input, and best practices for writing secure JavaScript code.

Common Security Vulnerabilities in JavaScript

1. **Cross-Site Scripting (XSS):**
    o **XSS** is one of the most common and dangerous security vulnerabilities in web applications. It occurs when an attacker injects malicious scripts (usually JavaScript) into web pages that are viewed by other users.

o Attackers can use XSS to steal session cookies, hijack user sessions, deface websites, and perform malicious actions on behalf of the victim.

2. **Cross-Site Request Forgery (CSRF)**:

o **CSRF** is an attack where a malicious website or script tricks a user into performing actions on a web application where they are authenticated. Since the request comes from the user's browser, it is often treated as legitimate, even though it was forged.

3. **SQL Injection**:

o While SQL injection is typically a backend security issue, poorly sanitized data passed to the server through JavaScript can be used to manipulate SQL queries and potentially expose sensitive data.

4. **Insecure Direct Object References (IDOR)**:

o This vulnerability occurs when an attacker is able to manipulate or predict the location of resources (such as files or database entries) and access them without proper authorization.

5. **Sensitive Data Exposure**:

o Storing sensitive data (like passwords, personal information, or authentication tokens) in insecure locations (such as **localStorage** or **sessionStorage**) or transmitting it without encryption can expose the data to attackers.

Preventing XSS (Cross-Site Scripting) Attacks

XSS attacks exploit the way that JavaScript interacts with the DOM, allowing attackers to inject malicious code into web pages. There are several strategies for preventing XSS attacks in your web applications.

1. **Sanitize User Input**: Ensure that all user input is sanitized before being inserted into the page. This means filtering out any potentially dangerous characters (like <, >, ", ', etc.) from input fields.

   Example (Sanitizing Input in JavaScript):

   javascript

   ```
   const userInput = document.getElementById('userInput').value;
   const sanitizedInput = userInput.replace(/[<>]/g, ''); // Removes < and > characters
   ```

2. **Escape Data**: Any dynamic data (such as user input or server response) that is inserted into HTML, JavaScript, or CSS should be properly escaped to ensure it cannot execute code.

   Example (Escaping HTML):

   javascript

```javascript
const input = '<script>alert("XSS Attack")</script>';
const escapedInput = input.replace(/</g, '&lt;').replace(/>/g, '&gt;');
document.getElementById('output').innerHTML = escapedInput;
```

3. **Use textContent or setAttribute Instead of innerHTML**: Avoid using innerHTML to insert user-generated content into the DOM, as it allows HTML and JavaScript code execution. Instead, use textContent or setAttribute, which automatically escapes HTML tags.

Example:

javascript

```javascript
const userContent = "<h1>Welcome</h1>";
const div = document.createElement('div');
div.textContent = userContent;  // Safely inserts text without interpreting HTML
document.body.appendChild(div);
```

4. **Content Security Policy (CSP)**: A **CSP** is a browser feature that helps detect and mitigate certain types of attacks, including XSS. By specifying which sources of content are allowed (scripts, images, etc.), you can prevent malicious code from executing.

Example (CSP Header):

http

Content-Security-Policy: default-src 'self'; script-src 'self' https://apis.google.com;

- o This policy only allows scripts from the same origin ('self') or from apis.google.com, preventing the execution of scripts from unauthorized sources.

Sanitizing User Input

Sanitizing user input is a fundamental practice to ensure that input data cannot be used to execute malicious actions, such as injecting harmful scripts or altering data. Always treat user input as untrusted and sanitize it before using it in your application.

1. **Sanitizing HTML Input**: If your application allows HTML input, use a library or service to sanitize the input before rendering it. The **DOMPurify** library is a popular choice for sanitizing HTML in the browser.

   Example (Using DOMPurify):

   javascript

   ```javascript
   // Include the DOMPurify library (either via CDN or npm)
   const sanitizedHTML = DOMPurify.sanitize(userInput);
   document.getElementById('content').innerHTML = sanitizedHTML;
   ```

2. **Avoid Inline JavaScript**: Inline JavaScript (such as onclick attributes) is vulnerable to XSS attacks. Always separate JavaScript from HTML and avoid using inline event handlers.

Example:

html

```
<!-- Unsafe (inline JavaScript) -->
<button onclick="alert('XSS Attack')">Click me</button>

<!-- Safe -->
<button id="clickButton">Click me</button>
<script>
  document.getElementById('clickButton').addEventListener('click',
function() {
    alert('Button clicked');
  });
</script>
```

Writing Secure JavaScript Code

To write secure JavaScript code, there are a few best practices you should follow to minimize security risks.

1. **Use HTTPS**: Always use **HTTPS** (instead of HTTP) to ensure that communication between the client and server is encrypted. This prevents man-in-the-middle attacks and

ensures that sensitive data (like login credentials) cannot be intercepted.

2. **Avoid Storing Sensitive Data in Local Storage**: While **localStorage** and **sessionStorage** are convenient, they are not secure for storing sensitive data like authentication tokens, passwords, or personal information. If you must store sensitive data in the browser, use **secure cookies** with the HttpOnly and Secure flags.

3. **Validate Input on Both Client and Server Side**: Never rely solely on client-side validation. Always validate and sanitize user input on the server side as well, as client-side validation can be bypassed by attackers.

4. **Use Secure Authentication Mechanisms**: Implement **JWT (JSON Web Tokens)** or **OAuth** for secure authentication. Avoid using basic authentication or passing plain credentials in URLs or HTTP headers.

5. **Use CSP and Other Security Headers**: Besides using **Content Security Policy (CSP)**, ensure that you implement other HTTP security headers such as **X-Content-Type-Options**, **X-XSS-Protection**, and **Strict-Transport-Security**.

6. **Limit Permissions**: Restrict the use of JavaScript features that can be exploited, such as eval(), setTimeout() with dynamic code, or accessing sensitive browser features unless absolutely necessary.

In this chapter, we explored **JavaScript security best practices** to protect your web applications from common vulnerabilities, including **XSS**, **CSRF**, and **SQL injection**. We covered strategies for preventing XSS attacks, such as **sanitizing user input**, **escaping data**, using **CSP** headers, and following secure coding practices. By understanding and implementing these practices, you can significantly reduce the risk of attacks and ensure the safety of your users and applications.

Writing secure JavaScript code is not just about defending against common vulnerabilities—it's about creating applications that prioritize user trust, privacy, and data integrity.

Chapter 23: JavaScript Performance Optimization

Performance optimization is a critical aspect of web development, especially as applications grow in complexity. JavaScript, being the primary language for building interactive web applications, plays a key role in ensuring smooth performance. In this chapter, we will dive into the common **JavaScript performance bottlenecks**, techniques to optimize JavaScript performance, the **event loop** and its role in concurrency, and how to profile and debug performance issues.

Understanding JavaScript Performance Bottlenecks

Performance bottlenecks occur when certain parts of your code or processes take longer to execute than others, slowing down the overall performance of your application. JavaScript, like any other language, has potential bottlenecks that you should be aware of.

1. **DOM Manipulation**:
   o **Heavy DOM interactions** (e.g., frequent updates to the DOM, especially with large web pages) can cause performance issues, as the browser needs to re-render

and repaint the DOM, which is an expensive operation.

- o Avoid direct manipulation of the DOM in a loop. Use methods like **document.createDocumentFragment()** or batch DOM updates to minimize reflows and repaints.

2. **Large JavaScript Files**:
- o Large and complex JavaScript files can slow down the initial loading of a webpage. Splitting large files into smaller, modular pieces and using **code-splitting** techniques (like those provided by **Webpack**) can improve performance.

3. **Blocking Code**:
- o **Synchronous blocking** operations (e.g., long-running loops or synchronous I/O operations) can block the JavaScript thread, preventing the browser from performing other tasks, such as rendering UI updates.
- o Use asynchronous methods such as **setTimeout()**, **setInterval()**, **Promises**, and **async/await** to prevent blocking.

4. **Memory Leaks**:
- o Memory leaks occur when objects are not properly cleaned up, causing your application to use more

memory than necessary, which can lead to slower performance over time.

- o Common causes include unused event listeners, circular references, or global variables that are never freed.

5. **Inefficient Loops and Algorithms**:

- o Loops or algorithms that do too much work or are not optimized can cause performance issues, especially with large datasets.

- o Use **efficient algorithms** and **loop optimization** techniques, such as reducing the number of iterations, caching values, or using better data structures like hashmaps.

Techniques for Optimizing JavaScript Performance

Here are some techniques to optimize the performance of your JavaScript code:

1. **Minimize DOM Access**:

- o Accessing and modifying the DOM is slow, so minimize DOM interactions.

- o Instead of repeatedly querying the DOM inside a loop, **cache DOM references** outside the loop.

- o Use **document fragments** for batch updates.

Example:

javascript

```javascript
const list = document.getElementById('list');
const fragment = document.createDocumentFragment();

// Batch updates to avoid multiple reflows
for (let i = 0; i < 1000; i++) {
    const listItem = document.createElement('li');
    listItem.textContent = `Item ${i}`;
    fragment.appendChild(listItem);
}

list.appendChild(fragment);  // Append all items in one go
```

2. **Debouncing and Throttling Events**:
   - o **Debouncing** and **throttling** are techniques to limit how often a function is invoked during events like **scrolling, typing**, or **window resizing**.
   - o **Debouncing** ensures that a function is executed only after a specified time interval after the last event.
   - o **Throttling** ensures that a function is executed only once in a specified time interval.

   Example (Debouncing):

   javascript

```
let debounceTimer;
const handleResize = () => {
  clearTimeout(debounceTimer);
  debounceTimer = setTimeout(() => {
    console.log('Resize event handled');
  }, 200);
};
```

```
window.addEventListener('resize', handleResize);
```

3. **Asynchronous Programming**:

   o Use **async/await** and **Promises** to perform non-blocking operations. This allows other tasks (like UI rendering) to continue while waiting for data or other tasks to complete.

   Example (Async/Await):

   javascript

```
const fetchData = async () => {
  try {
    const response = await fetch('https://api.example.com/data');
    const data = await response.json();
    console.log(data);
  } catch (error) {
    console.error('Error fetching data', error);
  }
};
```

fetchData();

4. **Lazy Loading**:

   o **Lazy loading** delays the loading of non-essential resources, such as images or modules, until they are needed. This can drastically improve initial load time.

   o You can use **IntersectionObserver** or **dynamic imports** for lazy loading.

   Example (Lazy Loading Images):

   javascript

   ```javascript
   const images = document.querySelectorAll('img[data-src]');
   const lazyLoad = () => {
     images.forEach(img => {
       if (img.getBoundingClientRect().top < window.innerHeight) {
         img.src = img.getAttribute('data-src');
         img.removeAttribute('data-src');
       }
     });
   };

   window.addEventListener('scroll', lazyLoad);
   lazyLoad(); // Initial check on page load
   ```

5. **Use Web Workers for Heavy Computations**:

- o **Web Workers** allow you to run scripts in the background on a separate thread, preventing them from blocking the main thread.
- o This is especially useful for heavy computations like sorting large datasets or performing image processing.

Example (Web Worker):

javascript

```
const worker = new Worker('worker.js');
worker.postMessage('Start processing');

worker.onmessage = (event) => {
    console.log('Processed result:', event.data);
};
```

The Event Loop and How JavaScript Handles Concurrency

JavaScript is **single-threaded**, meaning it can only execute one operation at a time. The **event loop** is responsible for handling asynchronous code, allowing JavaScript to perform non-blocking operations (like I/O or waiting for a response from a network request) while still being able to run other code.

1. **How the Event Loop Works:**

o When JavaScript runs, it executes synchronous code first, line by line. Once all synchronous code has been executed, it checks the **event queue** for any asynchronous code (like callbacks, promises, etc.).

o **Tasks** like event handlers, promises, and I/O operations are placed into the event queue, which the event loop processes when the main stack is empty.

2. **JavaScript Concurrency Model**:

o The **call stack** stores the functions currently being executed.

o The **event loop** checks if the call stack is empty and if so, moves tasks from the event queue to the stack.

o **Web APIs** like setTimeout() and fetch() enable asynchronous operations by handing off tasks to the browser's API, which executes them in the background and pushes the result to the event queue.

3. **Microtasks and Macrotasks**:

o **Microtasks** (such as Promise.then() handlers) are executed before **macrotasks** (such as setTimeout()) in the event loop, even if the macrotasks are queued first.

• **Example**:

javascript

```
console.log('Start');

setTimeout(() => {
    console.log('Macrotask: setTimeout');
}, 0);

Promise.resolve().then(() => {
    console.log('Microtask: Promise');
});

console.log('End');
```

Output:

```vbnet

Start
End
Microtask: Promise
Macrotask: setTimeout
```

o   This shows that microtasks are executed before macrotasks, even if the macrotasks are queued first.

Profiling and Debugging Performance Issues

To effectively optimize performance, you must first identify where the bottlenecks are. Profiling and debugging tools in modern browsers help you track performance and pinpoint slow areas in your code.

1. **Using Chrome DevTools**:
   - Chrome DevTools provides several tools for profiling performance, including the **Performance panel**, **Memory panel**, and **Lighthouse**.
   - **Performance Panel**: Helps you measure the performance of your code by showing a timeline of events, script executions, and layout recalculations.
     - Open the Performance panel (Ctrl+Shift+I > Performance) and click "Record" to start profiling. Perform the actions you want to measure and stop recording to analyze the results.
   - **Lighthouse**: Provides an automated report of performance, accessibility, SEO, and best practices.
     - Open the **Lighthouse** tab in Chrome DevTools and run an audit to get performance suggestions.

2. **Identifying Memory Leaks**:
   - The **Memory panel** helps you track memory usage and detect potential memory leaks.
   - You can take a heap snapshot and analyze the memory allocation to find objects that should have been garbage collected but haven't been.

3. **Using console.time() for Measuring Code Performance**:

o The console.time() and console.timeEnd() methods allow you to measure how long a block of code takes to execute.

Example:

javascript

```
console.time('sort');
const sortedArray = array.sort();
console.timeEnd('sort');  // Output: sort: <time in ms>
```

In this chapter, we explored JavaScript **performance optimization techniques**, focusing on identifying common performance bottlenecks, improving DOM manipulation, reducing memory usage, and using asynchronous programming to handle concurrency. We also discussed the **event loop** and how JavaScript handles concurrency in a single-threaded environment. Profiling and debugging tools such as **Chrome DevTools** and **Lighthouse** are essential for identifying and addressing performance issues in your code. By applying these optimization techniques and practices, you can build fast, responsive web applications that deliver a great user experience.

Chapter 24: Testing and Debugging JavaScript

Testing and debugging are essential skills for any JavaScript developer. Writing tests ensures that your code works as expected, while debugging helps you find and fix errors during development. In this chapter, we will cover the importance of testing in JavaScript, how to write unit tests using popular testing frameworks like **Jest** and **Mocha**, debugging techniques using browser development tools, and integrating **Continuous Integration (CI)** into JavaScript applications.

Importance of Testing in JavaScript

Testing is a critical practice in software development that helps ensure code quality, stability, and functionality. For JavaScript, testing is especially important due to the dynamic nature of the language, and the variety of environments in which JavaScript runs (web browsers, Node.js, etc.). Without proper testing, bugs and errors can go undetected, leading to performance issues or even security vulnerabilities.

Benefits of Testing:

- **Catches Bugs Early**: Automated tests help identify issues early in the development process.

- **Improves Code Quality**: Writing tests forces developers to write cleaner, more modular code.

- **Refactoring Confidence**: Tests give developers confidence when refactoring or adding new features, ensuring that existing functionality is not broken.

- **Documentation**: Tests act as a form of documentation, explaining how a function or module is expected to behave.

Writing Unit Tests with Testing Frameworks (Jest, Mocha)

Unit testing is the process of testing individual units or components of code (such as functions or methods) in isolation from the rest of the application. JavaScript provides several testing frameworks that help automate and structure unit tests.

1. **Jest**:
   - Jest is a popular testing framework developed by Facebook, primarily used with React but compatible with any JavaScript project.
   - It provides an easy-to-use API, supports snapshots, and comes with built-in mocking, spying, and assertion libraries.

o   Jest is commonly used for unit tests, integration tests, and end-to-end tests.

Example (Jest Unit Test):

javascript

```
// Function to test
function add(a, b) {
   return a + b;
}


// Jest test case
test('adds two numbers', () => {
   expect(add(2, 3)).toBe(5);
});
```

Running Jest Tests:

o   Install Jest via npm:

bash

```
npm install --save-dev jest
```

o   Add a test script in your package.json:

json

```
"scripts": {
   "test": "jest"
```

```
}
```

- o Run the tests using npm test.

2. **Mocha**:

- o Mocha is another popular JavaScript testing framework that provides a flexible and extensible environment for running tests.

- o Mocha can be used with other assertion libraries like **Chai** and **Sinon** for more advanced testing features (such as spies and mocks).

Example (Mocha Unit Test):

javascript

```javascript
const assert = require('assert');

// Function to test
function subtract(a, b) {
   return a - b;
}

// Mocha test case
describe('subtract()', function() {
   it('should subtract two numbers correctly', function() {
      assert.equal(subtract(5, 3), 2);
   });
});
```

Running Mocha Tests:

o Install Mocha via npm:

bash

npm install --save-dev mocha

o Add a test script in your package.json:

json

```
"scripts": {
    "test": "mocha"
}
```

o Run the tests using npm test.

3. **Mocking and Spying**:

o Both Jest and Mocha (with Sinon) allow you to mock or spy on functions to test interactions, ensuring that the correct functions are called with the correct arguments.

Example (Mocking with Jest):

javascript

```
const fetchData = jest.fn(() => Promise.resolve('data'));

test('fetches data', async () => {
  const data = await fetchData();
  expect(fetchData).toHaveBeenCalled();
```

```
        expect(data).toBe('data');
    });
```

Debugging Techniques Using Browser Dev Tools

Debugging is the process of identifying and fixing errors in your code. **Browser DevTools** provide a powerful set of tools for inspecting, testing, and debugging JavaScript code directly in the browser.

1. **Setting Breakpoints**:
   - o Breakpoints allow you to pause the execution of your code at a specific line, enabling you to inspect variables and step through the code.
   - o In Chrome DevTools, open the **Sources** tab, navigate to your JavaScript file, and click on the line number where you want to set a breakpoint.

2. **Using the Console**:
   - o The **Console** is one of the most widely used debugging tools, where you can log values and messages to track the execution of your code.
   - o You can use console.log(), console.table(), console.error(), and other logging methods to output data to the console.

Example:

javascript

```
const result = add(2, 3);
console.log('Addition result:', result);
```

3. **Watch Expressions**:
   - In Chrome DevTools, the **Watch** panel allows you to monitor specific variables or expressions in real time as you step through the code.

4. **Call Stack and Scope**:
   - The **Call Stack** shows you the functions that have been called up to the current point, helping you understand the flow of execution.
   - The **Scope** panel shows the current values of variables in the current function scope, enabling you to inspect the state of your application during debugging.

5. **Network Panel**:
   - The **Network Panel** is used to monitor all network requests (such as API calls) made by the application. You can inspect the response, request headers, and status codes to debug any issues with network interactions.

6. **Performance Panel**:
   - The **Performance Panel** allows you to record and analyze performance bottlenecks, such as slow

scripts or rendering issues. This is useful for optimizing the performance of your JavaScript code.

Continuous Integration for JavaScript Applications

Continuous Integration (CI) is a practice where developers frequently integrate their code into a shared repository. This process involves automating the testing, building, and deployment of code to ensure that it remains stable as changes are made. CI helps identify bugs early and ensures that code is always in a deployable state.

1. **Setting Up CI with GitHub Actions**: GitHub Actions is a popular CI/CD service that allows you to automate workflows directly in GitHub repositories.

   Example (GitHub Actions CI Workflow): Create a .github/workflows/ci.yml file in your repository:

   ```yaml
   yaml

   name: JavaScript CI

   on:
     push:
       branches:
         - main
     pull_request:
   ```

```
      branches:
       - main

    jobs:
     test:
      runs-on: ubuntu-latest
      steps:
       - name: Checkout code
         uses: actions/checkout@v2
       - name: Set up Node.js
         uses: actions/setup-node@v2
         with:
          node-version: '14'
       - name: Install dependencies
         run: npm install
       - name: Run tests
         run: npm test
```

- o This configuration automatically runs tests every time code is pushed or a pull request is made to the main branch.

- o The **GitHub Actions** workflow installs dependencies and runs the tests using your existing testing script (e.g., npm test).

2. **Other CI Services**:

- o **Travis CI**, **CircleCI**, and **GitLab CI** are other CI tools that can be configured to run JavaScript tests automatically when code changes are made.

3. **Benefits of CI**:

   o **Automation**: Automatically run tests and build scripts without manual intervention.

   o **Faster Feedback**: Get immediate feedback when new changes are made, reducing the time between writing code and finding bugs.

   o **Improved Code Quality**: With automated testing, you can ensure that your code is stable and meets quality standards.

In this chapter, we explored **testing** and **debugging** practices for JavaScript, focusing on the importance of testing, writing unit tests with frameworks like **Jest** and **Mocha**, and debugging using browser development tools. We also covered the concept of **Continuous Integration (CI)**, which helps automate testing and deployment processes to ensure that your codebase remains stable and reliable. By adopting these practices, you can improve the quality and maintainability of your JavaScript applications, ensuring that they perform as expected and are free from bugs.

Chapter 25: JavaScript and the Server-Side: Node.js

Node.js has revolutionized the way JavaScript is used in web development by enabling developers to write server-side code in JavaScript. It allows you to use JavaScript not just in the browser but also on the server, creating a unified development experience across both client-side and server-side. In this chapter, we will introduce you to **Node.js**, explain how to set up a Node.js server, build a simple **REST API**, and work with **Express.js** to handle HTTP requests.

Introduction to Node.js and Server-Side JavaScript

Node.js is an open-source, cross-platform runtime environment that allows you to run JavaScript code on the server side. It uses the **V8 JavaScript engine** (the same engine used by Google Chrome) to execute code, and it provides APIs to interact with the file system, network, and other low-level tasks commonly associated with server-side programming.

Unlike traditional web servers that use languages like PHP, Python, or Ruby, Node.js allows developers to use JavaScript across both the client and server, leading to faster development cycles and the ability to share code between the client and server.

Key Features of Node.js:

- **Non-blocking I/O**: Node.js uses asynchronous, event-driven programming, making it highly efficient for handling many concurrent requests.
- **Single-threaded**: Node.js runs on a single thread but uses an event loop to handle multiple tasks concurrently.
- **npm (Node Package Manager)**: Node.js has a robust package ecosystem that allows you to easily install and use libraries and frameworks like **Express.js**, **MongoDB**, and **Socket.io**.

Setting Up a Node.js Server

To start using Node.js, you first need to install it on your system.

1. **Installing Node.js**:
   - Go to the official Node.js website and download the latest stable version for your operating system.
   - After installation, you can verify that Node.js is installed correctly by running the following commands in your terminal:

   bash

```
node -v  # Check the installed Node.js version
npm -v   # Check the installed npm version
```

2. **Creating a Simple Node.js Server**: Once Node.js is installed, you can create a simple HTTP server.

Example (Simple Node.js HTTP Server):

javascript

```javascript
// app.js
const http = require('http');

const server = http.createServer((req, res) => {
    res.statusCode = 200;  // Set status code to 200 (OK)
    res.setHeader('Content-Type', 'text/plain');   // Set response content
type
    res.end('Hello, Node.js!');  // Send response body
});

server.listen(3000, 'localhost', () => {
    console.log('Server is running at http://localhost:3000/');
});
```

- o This server listens on port 3000 and responds with "Hello, Node.js!" to every request.

To run the server, use the command:

bash

node app.js

- o Open your browser and visit http://localhost:3000/ to see the response.

Building a Simple REST API with Node.js

REST (Representational State Transfer) is an architectural style for building web services. With Node.js, you can easily create a RESTful API that listens for HTTP requests and sends back responses in formats like JSON.

1. **Creating a Simple REST API**: Let's build a basic REST API that responds to **GET**, **POST**, **PUT**, and **DELETE** requests.

   Example (Simple REST API):

   javascript

   ```javascript
   const http = require('http');
   const url = require('url');

   const server = http.createServer((req, res) => {
       const parsedUrl = url.parse(req.url, true);

       // Set headers
   ```

```javascript
    res.statusCode = 200;
    res.setHeader('Content-Type', 'application/json');

    // Handle different HTTP methods and routes
    if (req.method === 'GET' && parsedUrl.pathname === '/api/greet') {
        const name = parsedUrl.query.name || 'World';
        res.end(JSON.stringify({ message: `Hello, ${name}!` }));
    } else if (req.method === 'POST' && parsedUrl.pathname ===
'/api/greet') {
        let body = '';
        req.on('data', chunk => {
            body += chunk;
        });
        req.on('end', () => {
            const data = JSON.parse(body);
            res.end(JSON.stringify({ message: `Hello, ${data.name}!` }));
        });
    } else {
        res.statusCode = 404;
        res.end(JSON.stringify({ message: 'Not Found' }));
    }
});

server.listen(3000, 'localhost', () => {
    console.log('Server running at http://localhost:3000/');
});
```

Explanation:

- o The **GET** request at /api/greet returns a greeting message, optionally personalized with a name query parameter.
- o The **POST** request at /api/greet expects a JSON body with a name field, and it responds with a personalized greeting.

Testing the API:

- o You can test the **GET** request with your browser or curl:

  bash

  ```
  curl "http://localhost:3000/api/greet?name=John"
  ```

- o For the **POST** request, you can use **Postman** or curl with JSON data:

  bash

  ```
  curl -X POST "http://localhost:3000/api/greet" -d '{"name":"Alice"}' -H "Content-Type: application/json"
  ```

Working with Express.js and Handling Requests

While building a Node.js server from scratch is useful for learning, **Express.js** simplifies the process of building web applications and APIs by providing a set of robust features and middleware.

1. **Setting Up Express.js**:
   - Express is a minimalist and flexible framework for building web applications in Node.js.
   - To install Express, run:

     bash

     npm install express

2. **Building a REST API with Express.js**: Here's how to create a simple REST API using **Express.js**:

   Example (Express.js REST API):

   javascript

```javascript
const express = require('express');
const app = express();

app.use(express.json());  // Middleware to parse JSON bodies

// GET request handler
app.get('/api/greet', (req, res) => {
    const name = req.query.name || 'World';
    res.json({ message: `Hello, ${name}!` });
```

```
});
```

```
// POST request handler
app.post('/api/greet', (req, res) => {
   const { name } = req.body;
   res.json({ message: `Hello, ${name}!` });
});
```

```
app.listen(3000, () => {
   console.log('Express server running at http://localhost:3000/');
});
```

Explanation:

- o The **GET** route responds with a greeting, similar to the previous example.
- o The **POST** route accepts a JSON body, extracting the name and responding with a personalized message.

3. **Middleware**:

- o Express allows you to use **middleware**, which are functions that execute during the request-response cycle. Middleware can be used to handle tasks such as logging, authentication, or body parsing.

Example (Logging Middleware):

javascript

```
app.use((req, res, next) => {
   console.log(`${req.method} ${req.url}`);
```

```
next(); // Pass control to the next middleware
});
```

4. **Handling Errors**:

   o You can define error-handling middleware in Express to catch and handle errors globally.

   Example (Error Handling Middleware):

   javascript

```
app.use((err, req, res, next) => {
  console.error(err.stack);
  res.status(500).json({ message: 'Something went wrong!' });
});
```

In this chapter, you've learned how to use **Node.js** to build server-side JavaScript applications. We started by setting up a basic Node.js server and created a simple REST API. Then, we introduced **Express.js**, which simplifies server-side development and routing, and showed how to handle various HTTP requests and responses using Express. By leveraging **Node.js** and **Express.js**, you can create fast, scalable web applications and APIs with JavaScript, making it a powerful tool for full-stack development.

Chapter 26: JavaScript in Mobile Development

JavaScript is not limited to web development; it can also be used to build mobile applications. With frameworks like **React Native**, JavaScript developers can leverage their existing skills to build cross-platform mobile applications that run on both **iOS** and **Android**. In this chapter, we will explore how JavaScript is used for mobile development, specifically with **React Native**, and cover how to build cross-platform mobile apps, work with mobile UI components and navigation, and debug and test mobile apps.

Using JavaScript for Mobile Apps with React Native

React Native is an open-source framework created by Facebook that allows you to build mobile applications using **JavaScript** and **React**. With React Native, you can write mobile apps for both iOS and Android using a single codebase. It provides a rich set of native components and APIs to access device capabilities like the camera, GPS, and sensors.

1. **Setting Up React Native**:
   - o To start building with React Native, you need to install **Node.js**, **npm**, and the **React Native CLI**.

- o **Install React Native CLI**:

  bash

  npm install -g react-native-cli

- o **Creating a New React Native Project**:

  bash

  ```
  npx react-native init MyApp
  cd MyApp
  npx react-native run-android  # For Android
  npx react-native run-ios      # For iOS (MacOS only)
  ```

2. **React Native Architecture**:
   - o React Native uses a **bridge** to communicate between JavaScript code and native platform components. The **JavaScript thread** communicates with the **native thread** using asynchronous messages, allowing for high performance.
   - o It provides built-in components like View, Text, Image, Button, and TextInput, which map to native UI elements.

3. **React Native vs. Web React**:
   - o While React Native shares many concepts with React (such as components, state, and props), it uses native components rather than HTML elements. For example, instead of <div>, you use <View>.

Example (Basic React Native Component):

javascript

```javascript
import React from 'react';
import { View, Text, StyleSheet } from 'react-native';

const App = () => {
  return (
    <View style={styles.container}>
      <Text>Hello, React Native!</Text>
    </View>
  );
};

const styles = StyleSheet.create({
  container: {
    flex: 1,
    justifyContent: 'center',
    alignItems: 'center',
    backgroundColor: '#fff',
  },
});

export default App;
```

- o This is a simple React Native component that renders a text element on the screen with some basic styling.

Building Cross-Platform Mobile Apps with JavaScript

One of the main advantages of using React Native is the ability to build cross-platform apps with a single codebase. This means you can deploy the same app to both **iOS** and **Android** without having to write separate code for each platform. However, there are some platform-specific differences that you need to account for.

1. **Writing Cross-Platform Code**:
   - React Native provides a lot of **platform-specific components** and modules, but you can also customize the UI for each platform using **Platform-specific code**.
   - You can use the Platform module to detect the platform and apply conditional styles or logic.

   Example (Platform-Specific Code):

   javascript

   ```javascript
   import { Platform, Text, View, StyleSheet } from 'react-native';

   const App = () => {
     return (
       <View style={styles.container}>
         <Text>
           {Platform.OS === 'ios' ? 'Running on iOS' : 'Running on Android'}
         </Text>
       </View>
   ```

```
);
};

const styles = StyleSheet.create({
  container: {
    flex: 1,
    justifyContent: 'center',
    alignItems: 'center',
  },
});

export default App;
```

2. **Handling Native Modules**:

   o React Native allows you to access **native APIs** for each platform. For example, you can access the **camera**, **location services**, **storage**, etc.

   o You can use third-party libraries like **React Navigation**, **React Native Maps**, or **React Native Camera**, which provide these native modules.

Mobile UI Components and Navigation

Building an intuitive and responsive mobile UI is crucial for a successful app. React Native provides built-in components, but you can also integrate third-party libraries to enhance the user experience.

1. **Mobile UI Components**:
   - o **Text**: Displays text in your app.
   - o **View**: A container for layout, similar to a <div> in web React.
   - o **Image**: Displays images on the screen.
   - o **TextInput**: A form element for gathering text input from the user.
   - o **Button**: A clickable button for triggering actions.
   - o **TouchableOpacity**: A wrapper for creating touchable elements with custom styles.

Example (Using Mobile UI Components):

javascript

```
import React from 'react';
import { View, Text, TextInput, Button, StyleSheet } from 'react-native';

const App = () => {
  return (
    <View style={styles.container}>
      <TextInput style={styles.input} placeholder="Enter text" />
      <Button title="Submit" onPress={() => alert('Button pressed!')} />
    </View>
  );
};

const styles = StyleSheet.create({
  container: {
```

```
    flex: 1,
    justifyContent: 'center',
    alignItems: 'center',
  },
  input: {
   height: 40,
   borderColor: 'gray',
   borderWidth: 1,
   marginBottom: 20,
   width: '80%',
   padding: 10,
  },
});
```

export default App;

2. **Navigation in React Native**:

   o For handling navigation between screens, **React Navigation** is the most popular library. It supports **stack navigation**, **tab navigation**, and **drawer navigation**.

   o Install React Navigation and its dependencies:

   bash

   ```
   npm install @react-navigation/native
   npm install @react-navigation/stack
   npm install react-native-gesture-handler react-native-reanimated
   ```

3. **Example (Navigation Setup)**:

```
4.  javascript
5.
6.  import React from 'react';
7.  import { createStackNavigator } from '@react-navigation/stack';
8.  import { NavigationContainer } from '@react-navigation/native';
9.  import { Button, View, Text } from 'react-native';
10.
11. const HomeScreen = ({ navigation }) => (
12.   <View>
13.     <Text>Home Screen</Text>
14.     <Button
15.       title="Go to Details"
16.       onPress={() => navigation.navigate('Details')}
17.     />
18.   </View>
19. );
20.
21. const DetailsScreen = () => (
22.   <View>
23.     <Text>Details Screen</Text>
24.   </View>
25. );
26.
27. const Stack = createStackNavigator();
28.
29. const App = () => (
30.   <NavigationContainer>
31.     <Stack.Navigator initialRouteName="Home">
32.       <Stack.Screen name="Home" component={HomeScreen} />
```

33.   <Stack.Screen name="Details" component={DetailsScreen} />

34.   </Stack.Navigator>

35.   </NavigationContainer>

36.   );

37.

38. export default App;

- o This example demonstrates basic stack navigation where you can navigate between the **Home** and **Details** screens.

Debugging and Testing Mobile Apps

Debugging and testing mobile apps is a crucial step to ensure they function as expected and provide a good user experience. React Native provides powerful tools for debugging and testing mobile apps.

1. **Debugging Mobile Apps**:
   - o **React Native Debugger**: You can use the React Native Debugger (based on **Redux DevTools**) for inspecting the state, actions, and network requests in your app.
   - o **Console Logs**: Use console.log() to print debug information in the development console.
   - o **Remote JS Debugging**: Enable **Remote Debugging** in the developer menu to run JavaScript code in

Chrome's DevTools for a more robust debugging experience.

2. **Testing Mobile Apps**:

   o **Jest** is commonly used for unit and integration testing in React Native.

   o **React Native Testing Library** helps you write tests that focus on the way the user interacts with your components.

Example (Jest Unit Test):

javascript

```
import React from 'react';
import { render } from '@testing-library/react-native';
import App from './App';

test('renders correctly', () => {
  const { getByText } = render(<App />);
  expect(getByText('Hello, React Native!')).not.toBeNull();
});
```

   o **E2E Testing**: **Detox** is a popular framework for end-to-end testing in React Native, allowing you to simulate real user interactions.

In this chapter, we explored **JavaScript in mobile development**, focusing on **React Native** as a framework for building cross-platform mobile apps. We covered how to set up a React Native project, build a basic mobile UI, implement navigation, and debug and test mobile apps. With React Native, JavaScript developers can leverage their existing skills to create robust, native-like mobile applications for both **iOS** and **Android**. The ability to share code across platforms is a key benefit, and with the tools and techniques discussed in this chapter, you can build, test, and deploy mobile apps efficiently.

Chapter 27: Future of JavaScript and Next Steps

JavaScript is one of the most dynamic and evolving programming languages, and as new features and capabilities are added, staying updated becomes essential for developers. In this final chapter, we will look at the **future of JavaScript**, what's coming in **ECMAScript 2025 and beyond**, how to keep up with the latest trends, the best resources for continued learning, and how to engage with the **JavaScript developer community**.

The Future of JavaScript: ECMAScript 2025 and Beyond

ECMAScript is the standard that JavaScript follows, and each year brings new features, improvements, and refinements to the language. The **ECMAScript 2025** specification, along with its ongoing evolution, will continue to build on JavaScript's capabilities.

1. **Emerging Features**:
   - **Top-Level Await**: The ability to use await at the top level in modules, which simplifies asynchronous code, especially for imports.
     - Example:

javascript

```
// Top-level await in ES2022
const data = await fetchData();
console.log(data);
```

o **Pattern Matching**: This is one of the proposed features, enabling pattern matching in JavaScript, making it easier to work with complex conditions and data structures like objects and arrays.

- Example:

javascript

```
switch (value) {
  case { x: 1, y: 2 }:
    console.log('Matched a point!');
    break;
}
```

o **Private Methods and Fields**: JavaScript classes will continue to evolve, with private methods and fields becoming standard in ES2025, making object-oriented programming more secure and encapsulated.

- Example:

javascript

```
class MyClass {
```

```
#privateField = 'secret';

#privateMethod() {
  console.log(this.#privateField);
}

publicMethod() {
  this.#privateMethod();
}
}
```

o **Record & Tuple**: A new primitive type for immutable data structures. This will help with performance and optimization in JavaScript.

- Example:

javascript

```
const record = #[1, 2, 3];
const tuple = #(10, 20);
```

2. **Improved Performance**:
   o As JavaScript applications become larger and more complex, the language will continue to improve its performance through features like **optimized garbage collection, smarter compilers**, and **better memory management**.

- o **WebAssembly (Wasm)** will continue to grow alongside JavaScript, allowing high-performance code to run alongside JavaScript, especially for computationally heavy tasks like video editing or 3D rendering.

3. **Concurrency and Multi-threading**:
   - o JavaScript will continue to improve its concurrency model, possibly with more integrated support for **parallel programming** and **multi-threading**. Features like **Web Workers** and **SharedArrayBuffer** will become more integrated into JavaScript.

Keeping Up with JavaScript Trends and New Features

JavaScript is constantly evolving, and keeping up with the latest trends and features is crucial to staying relevant as a developer. Here's how you can keep up:

1. **Follow the ECMAScript Proposals**:
   - o The ECMAScript proposals process allows developers to track new features and improvements that are being discussed and tested for future versions of JavaScript. You can find detailed information on the TC39 GitHub repository.

2. **Stay Updated with the JavaScript Release Cycle**:

   o ECMAScript features are typically introduced in a regular cycle. New versions of ECMAScript are released annually, and keeping track of new updates can help you integrate new features into your workflow.

   o Follow official announcements on ECMA International and MDN Web Docs.

3. **Explore Frameworks and Libraries**:

   o JavaScript libraries and frameworks evolve alongside the language. **React**, **Vue.js**, **Angular**, **Svelte**, and **Node.js** frequently release new versions that take advantage of new JavaScript features.

   o Experiment with new libraries, frameworks, and tools in your side projects to understand how they leverage the latest JavaScript features.

4. **Read Blogs and Newsletters**:

   o Subscribe to JavaScript newsletters such as **JavaScript Weekly** and **JavaScript on Twitter** to stay informed about new trends, tutorials, and best practices.

   o Follow influential developers, companies, and JavaScript communities to get insights on industry trends.

5. **Online Resources and Courses**:

o **MDN Web Docs**: The official Mozilla Developer Network provides the most comprehensive resources on JavaScript.

o **JavaScript30**: A 30-day challenge to build JavaScript projects from scratch with vanilla JavaScript, focusing on pure JS skills.

o Platforms like **FreeCodeCamp**, **Udemy**, **Codecademy**, and **Egghead.io** offer courses on modern JavaScript development.

Recommended Resources for Continued Learning

To continue your journey as a JavaScript developer, consider the following resources:

1. **Books**:

   o *"You Don't Know JS"* by Kyle Simpson: A series of deep dives into JavaScript, focusing on the intricacies of the language.

   o *"Eloquent JavaScript"* by Marijn Haverbeke: An excellent resource for understanding JavaScript concepts and practical coding exercises.

   o *"JavaScript: The Good Parts"* by Douglas Crockford: A concise book focusing on the most elegant parts of JavaScript.

2. **Documentation**:

   o **MDN Web Docs**: The go-to place for detailed documentation on JavaScript, including language features, APIs, and examples.

   o **JavaScript.info**: A thorough guide and tutorial for both beginners and advanced developers.

3. **Online Communities**:

   o **Stack Overflow**: A platform to ask and answer programming questions.

   o **GitHub**: Explore open-source projects and contribute to the JavaScript ecosystem.

   o **Reddit**: Join JavaScript-focused subreddits such as **r/javascript, r/reactjs**, and **r/node**.

   o **Dev.to**: A platform where developers share articles, tutorials, and coding challenges.

4. **Podcasts**:

   o **JavaScript Jabber**: A podcast that discusses JavaScript and web development with industry experts.

   o **The Changelog**: Covers a variety of open-source topics, including JavaScript.

   o **Frontend Happy Hour**: Focuses on frontend development, including React, JavaScript, and other web technologies.

Joining the JavaScript Developer Community

The JavaScript community is vast, welcoming, and vibrant, providing numerous opportunities to learn, share knowledge, and collaborate on projects.

1. **Contributing to Open-Source**:
   - Contributing to open-source JavaScript projects on platforms like GitHub is a great way to improve your skills, collaborate with others, and gain recognition in the community.
   - Many popular JavaScript libraries, frameworks, and tools are open-source, and contributions are always welcome.

2. **Attending Meetups and Conferences**:
   - **Meetups**: Join local or virtual JavaScript meetups where developers gather to discuss new technologies, frameworks, and best practices.
   - **Conferences**: Attend JavaScript conferences such as **JSConf, ReactConf, NodeConf,** and **Frontend Conf** to hear from industry leaders, network with peers, and learn the latest in JavaScript development.

3. **Mentorship and Pair Programming**:

- o Join online platforms such as **Exercism**, **Codewars**, or **LeetCode** to practice coding challenges and connect with mentors.
- o Pair programming, whether in-person or remotely, helps you improve your problem-solving skills and collaborate with others.

4. **Online Forums and Discussion Boards**:
- o Participate in discussions on forums such as **Stack Overflow**, **Dev.to**, **GitHub Discussions**, and **Reddit**. Ask questions, share insights, and engage with developers from around the world.

The **future of JavaScript** is filled with exciting developments and continuous evolution. ECMAScript 2025 and beyond will bring more powerful features to improve performance, usability, and developer experience. By keeping up with the latest trends, continuing to learn from reputable resources, and engaging with the JavaScript community, you can stay at the forefront of this ever-evolving language. The journey of learning JavaScript is ongoing, and as you progress, you will contribute to and benefit from the wealth of knowledge that exists in the JavaScript ecosystem. Happy coding!